EVERYMAN,
I WILL GO WITH THEE,
AND BE THY GUIDE,
IN THY MOST NEED
TO GO BY THY SIDE

SANDRA CISNEROS

THE HOUSE ON MANGO STREET

WITH AN INTRODUCTION
BY JOHN PHILLIP SANTOS

EVERYMAN'S LIBRARY
Alfred A. Knopf New York London Toronto

everymanslibrary.com
www.everymanslibrary.co.uk

ISBN: 978-1-101-90846-4 (US)
978-1-84159-423-1 (UK)

A CIP catalogue reference for this book is available from the
British Library

Typography by Peter B. Willberg

Book design by Barbara de Wilde and Carol Devine Carson

Typeset in the UK by Input Data Services Ltd, Bridgwater, Somerset

Printed and bound in Germany by GGP Media GmbH, Pössneck

THE HOUSE ON
MANGO STREET

When we meet Esperanza Cordero, the almost mystically know-ing young Chicana narrator of *The House on Mango Street*, she is already very much a canny teller of tales, speaking *in medias res*, in the midst of an unfolding story of her heroic quest to find a true home.

"We didn't always live on Mango Street," she begins.

She details a litany of her family's *peregrinajes* through previous houses in Chicago, as if reading from some codex memorializing a series of sacred migrations:

"Before that we lived on Loomis on the third floor, and before that we lived on Keeler. Before Keeler it was Paulina, and before that I can't remember. But what I remember is moving a lot. Each time it seemed there'd be one more of us. By the time we got to Mango Street we were six – Mama, Papa, Carlos, Kiki, my sister Nenny and me."

Involuntary peregrinations and deprivations spark Esper-anza's imagination. Her family has had to leave their previous residence when the "water pipes broke and the landlord wouldn't fix them because the house was too old. We had to leave fast." Esperanza dreams of a house with "running water and pipes that worked." She imagines a house with "three washrooms so when we took a bath we wouldn't have to tell everybody." It would be a white house, surrounded by a proper yard with trees and grass. "This was the house Papa talked about when he held a lottery ticket and this was the house Mama dreamed up in the stories she told us before we went to bed."

But as Esperanza candidly reveals, the family's new house on Mango Street only has one bathroom, and "Everybody has to share a bedroom – Mama and Papa, Carlos and Kiki, me and Nenny."

"I knew then I had to have a house. A real house. One I could point to. But this isn't it. The house on Mango Street isn't it." And then, fathoming her disappointment and longing, Esperanza takes us into her confidence, she shares something that is beyond an intuition – it's a glimpse at a secret, deeper

knowing of unknown origin that will propel and inflect the un-
forgettable stories that are to come: "For the time being, Mama
says. Temporary, says Papa. But I know how those things go."

How can she know this? How can such *she* already know *the
way things go*? And why is she offering us her *testimonio*?

It's Esperanza's ineluctable knowing and her indelible way of
expressing it which transfixes readers around the globe with a
universal human story of a young girl's becoming, establishing
The House on Mango Street over decades as the first Latinx American classic of world letters. Seven million copies have been sold
in the United States, and millions more abroad, in as many as
twenty-six translations. Notably, it is also the first book by a US-
born Latinx writer to be included in the legendary and august
Everyman's Library series, auspicious indeed for the author and
the book – as well as for the series. And as celebrated as the novel
has been in the forty years since its publication, it's important to
point out that despite wide adoption in school curricula, it has
also been banned from schools in numerous flashpoints during
America's recent and ongoing culture wars, officially cited for
"age appropriateness" – but it's Esperanza's searing powers of
observation, and her "knowing" of the world around her, especially coming from a young Chicana, that seem to strike fear in
some people's hearts.

As the author of *The House on Mango Street*, Sandra Cisneros
brings a profound new embrace of a unique literary legacy of the
Americas to the Everyman series, as an American writer who
is *mestiza*, *feminista*, *urbana*, *cosmopolitana*, and *sin vergüenza* – all
without shame.

Esperanza's limpid voice, her deceptively simple diction, her
unique lyrical vernacular, belie a profound understanding of
the complex intricacies of our humanity that can't be fully explained, but it has deep roots in the experiences, readings, and
understandings of the author, herself an oracle of a knowing that
eludes explanation.

*

I met Sandra Cisneros in my hometown of San Antonio, Texas
in 1983, just before the publication of *The House on Mango Street* by
a small Latino publishing house in Houston, Arte Público Press,

that first published works of now well-known Latinx writers, as well as "lost" Latinx literary works. Vivacious, loquacious, and audacious, with an electric halo of ebony curls, she was by then entirely a protean whirlwind of literary marvel. She was just back from a walkabout across Europe (including four months in Yugoslavia), and the Mediterranean. Both of us were aspiring writers, but her aspirations were feverishly inquisitive, passionate and opinionated, volubly rooted in a commitment to writing as an act of bounding invention, and social conscience. A poet and fiction writer, she possessed a documentary eye that saw the many ways the world oppressed the poor and the marginalized.

She was a force unlike any I'd yet encountered, determined to use her gifts to sow new seeds in the fallow fields of American letters, so long ignorant and dismissive of voices like hers. And Chicanx letters, the work of Mexican American writers, were in an uncertain, in-between moment, emerging from a rich *movimiento* history into we-knew-not-yet what was to come.

As fate would have it, we were the finalists to become the inaugural Director of the literature program at the Guadalupe Cultural Arts Center, a newly created haven for Mexican American arts, literature, music, and theater in my hometown of San Antonio. Sandra (forgive the familiarity, but to refer to her any other way feels fake) got the job, but in meeting her then, I gained a lifelong literary ally, interlocutor, mentor, and occasional conspirator.

I had learned much from powerful women writers. I grew up with the poet Naomi Shihab Nye, had carried on a fraught correspondence with Laura (Riding) Jackson, and now Sandra arrived in San Antonio with a spell-binding sense of her own destiny, a destiny that would shortly unfold further in grand ways that were somehow against all odds while possessing a certain inevitability. She was an inspiration, and indeed, in three-hundred-year-old San Antonio she would eventually become *La Sandra,* a transforming presence for the city, and eventually for American literature.

It would take a while yet for the world to fully take note of *The House on Mango Street*, the mesmerizing *testimonio* of the journey of Esperanza Cordero among the souls and spaces of her Chicago neighborhood, as she struggles to assert her place in the world, as she longs for the dreamed-of house of her own. The path of this now universally classic novel to this Everyman's Library edition would be lengthy, and bumpy.

After the book's initial publication by the Houston small press, Sandra met her agent and forever since dharma companion Susan Bergholz. It was with the eventual publication of *The House on Mango Street* by Vintage Books in 1989 that the novel would begin to find its staggering, first national, then ever-widening global readership. But that wasn't thanks to any career-forging reviews in major newspapers or literary journals, virtually all of whom maintained their studied inattention and ignored the book. I remember it more as a gradually rising tide of word-of-mouth revelations, people passing the book along to one another like the talisman of a new reckoning with ourselves.

Like my thirteen-year-old daughter Francesca, who recently read the copy I handed her for the first time, after which she shared: "As a young Latina who is still figuring out everything, this book gave me so many ways to relate to the young protagonist. I saw myself in her, and I think many other girls my age could too. The feeling of not wanting to be contained – to not be limited to the things we get to do, say, or experience. The longing for more is something I cannot only greatly appreciate, but also deeply understand. I loved this book because usually when adults try to get into the minds of children, it's a colossal fail. It's unrealistic – and can even feel like they're mocking us. It just doesn't sit right. Sandra goes into the minds of children in a realistic way, adding beautiful touches of vibrant culture that makes me proud to be a Mexican American."

You get it? Literally millions have shared this experience, and this is a book that continues to light up souls.

When *The House on Mango Street* first appeared, we were in an interregnum period in Chicanx letters, uncertain about where our voices fit in the American, or for that matter, global literary epics. We were inheritors of a Mestizo saga that began long ago in Mexico. Some of us lived in parts of the United States that *were* once Mexico, and our ancestors saw their lands become another nation overnight. Others of us were legatees of myriad diasporas, migrations and other species of dispossession, fleeing war, fleeing poverty, eventually finding our way to American cities that had never known *mexicanos*.

There's a story of the origins of Mexican American literature that begins dually with the streams of Spanish letters alongside the unique literary legacies of the Mesoamerican indigenous peoples, whose painted books, detailing their origins, migrations, and interactions with gods and strangers, were nearly all burned by the Spanish conquistadores. José Martí once wrote that with those fires, the invaders "stole a page from the universe." We were born out of loss and longing.

Spanish, indigenous, and mestizo scribes and friars assembled the encyclopedic Florentine Codex, preserving some of the knowledge and cosmology of the Aztec world before the debacle, rendering all that knowing in Nahuatl, Spanish, and intricate imagery. Many scribes would follow, setting out into the vast dominions of *Nueva España*. This is a very short version of a much longer telling of all that we carry. That literary energy, full of memory, imagination, and inner spiritual conflict, traversed the centuries into the Chicano world we inherited, whether in San Antonio, Los Angeles, or Chicago.

"I'm of the Américas, north and south," as Sandra described herself in a recent conversation, living now for some years in San Miguel de Allende, Mexico, after her decades-long sojourn in San Antonio.

The *Movimiento*, the Chicano civil rights movement of the late '60s and early '70s saw a pivotal awakening of literary creativity, especially across the American Southwest. Largely male *Movimiento*-era writers such as Rodolfo Corky Gonzalez, in his poem of 1967, "I Am Joaquín," urged us to ask what it meant to be American as Mexicanos born in the United States, or descended from those who had immigrated from Mexico, like Sandra's father who went from Mexico City to Chicago:

I am Joaquín, lost in a world of confusion,
caught up in the whirl of a gringo society,
confused by the rules, scorned by attitudes,
suppressed by manipulation, and destroyed by modern society.

As playwright and director Luís Valdez put it, ". . . *being Chicano* means the utilization of one's total potentialities in the liberation of our people. In another sense, it means that Indio mysticism is merging with modern technology to create *un nuevo hombre*. A new man." There had been earlier fictional accounts of Chicanos coming of age, Tomás Rivera's . . . *And the Earth Did Not Swallow Him* (1971), Rudolfo Anaya's *Bless Me Ultima* (1972), or José Antonio Villaréal's *Pocho* (1959), but they weren't widely known beyond Chicanx cognoscenti.

Perhaps the earlier insurgencies of masculine Chicano urgency and nationalist anxiety allowed writers like Sandra in the late 1970s and early '80s to explore what it meant *to be human* as Mexican Americans. New orientations were emerging in the struggle. The movement was taking a spiritual, and decidedly more feminist turn, awakening to experiences of gender and sexuality in shaping who we are.

It was an impulse that would be taken up by a host of Chicana writers who would fundamentally change our literary landscape. Writing retrospectively, in the third person, about the period when she was composing *The House on Mango Street,* Sandra has said of herself and her other rebel literary peers: "Gloria Anzaldúa and Cherríe Moraga are cutting their own paths through the world somewhere, but she doesn't know about them . . . She's making things up as she goes."

Though she was officially writing poetry at the famous Iowa Writers' Workshop in 1977 (with Rita Dove and Joy Harjo as the only writers of color alongside her), Sandra began writing some of the pieces that would later become parts of *The House on Mango Street* there, completing the book during her European journey in 1982. Of that time, Sandra recalls, "How can art make a difference in the world? This was never asked at Iowa . . . At Iowa we never talked about serving others with our writing. It was all about serving ourselves."

She attributes some of her feminist *concientizacíon* as a writer at this time to meeting poet, author, editor, lifetime friend, Norma Alarcón, who introduced Sandra to such voices as Sor Juana Inés de la Cruz, Elena Poniatowska, Elena Garro, and Rosario Casteallanos. She credits Alarcón with convening an invisible college of Chicana writers: Cherríe Moraga, Gloria

Anzaldúa, Ana Castillo, Marjorie Agosín, Carla Trujillo, Diana Solís, Sandra Maria Esteves, Diane Gómez, Salima Rivera, Margarita López, Beatriz Badikian, Carmen Ábrego, Denise Chávez, Helena María Viramontes. Sandra remembers this time as "looking for another way to be – '*otro modo de ser*' . . . we had no idea what we were doing was extraordinary."

Of composing *The House on Mango Street* in that time, she says, "Sometimes I write about people I remember, sometimes I write about people I've just met, often I mix the two together." As *sui generis* as her novel's literary form appears, Sandra has literary and mythic precursors, some of whom she has named: Hans Christian Andersen, Lewis Carroll, and Jorge Luis Borges, all writers who saw history through a lens of the ineffable. Perhaps literati with Chicagoan tunings will also hear echoes of Carl Sandburg's timeless eloquence, the poetic diction of Gwendolyn Brooks, or the rich oral histories of Sandra's esteemed mentor Studs Terkel.

Writing again in the third person, she says of herself back then, "She experiments, creating a text that is as succinct and flexible as poetry, snapping sentences into fragments so that the reader pauses, making each sentence serve *her* and not the other way round, abandoning quotation marks to streamline the typography and make the page as simple and readable as possible. So that the sentences are pliant as branches and can be read in more ways than one." And also, "She *doesn't* want to write a book that a reader won't understand and would feel ashamed for not understanding."

Her Chicago, though it is unnamed throughout the book, is drawn in quick brush-strokes: "We ride fast and faster. Past my house, sad and red and crumbly in places, past Mr. Benny's grocery on the corner, and down the avenue which is dangerous. Laundromat, junk store, drugstore, windows and cars and more cars, and around the block back to Mango."

Sandra has explained how she lets her stories manifest their pacing, their beginnings and endings: "They're stubborn. They know best when there's no more to be said. The last sentence must ring like the final notes at the end of a mariachi song – *tan tán* – to tell you when the song is done."

And in the book's most menacing scene for Esperanza, our

author evokes the darkness through briefest details: "He said I love you, Spanish girl, I love you, and pressed his sour mouth to mine . . . Please don't make me tell it all."

Reading *The House on Mango Street* today, I'm struck by Esperanza's mediumistic qualities, which have taken me all these years to recognize. It's not magic realism, it's real magic. As in spirit mediumship, as in an inward ability to enter into the minds of others, or, as Sandra has described her process of writing, to "listen to the voices inside herself." Esperanza is searching for her home, but she is also coming to terms with her extraordinary powers, and she is doing so through writing. Her quest is spiritistic in nature, she is mastering immaterial forces within her.

"I put it down on paper and then the ghost does not ache so much. I write it down and Mango says goodbye sometimes. She does not hold me with both arms. She sets me free."

Sandra has written recently of her teacher, the late Thich Nhat Hanh's call to become "spiritual revolutionaries." She has described herself as a "Buddhalupista," merging Buddhism practice and reverence for the Virgen de Guadalupe. I now see the stirrings of that dharma in Esperanza, most powerfully in the climactic scene near the novel's end when she encounters the three mystic sisters who deliver an oracle: "When you leave you must remember to come back for the others. A circle, understand? You will always be Esperanza. You will always be Mango Street. You can't erase what you know. You can't forget who you are."

When I first met Sandra in San Antonio, she was living in a humble *casita*, a spare, true writer's garret in the backyard of a downtown house. Later, Esperanza's dream would come true and she'd find her first real house of her own, the legendary Casa Xóchitl. Benevolent and feverishly curious readers, spiritual seekers, will seek out Sandra Cisneros's poems, stories, memoirs, and her epic multi-generational novel, *Caramelo,* itself full of spirits and voices. In *The House on Mango Street* we find the beginning of a profound spiritual journey of becoming that is still unfolding.

John Phillip Santos

SELECT BIBLIOGRAPHY

SALDÍVAR-HULL, SONIA, *Feminism on the Border: Chicana Gender Politics and Literature*, University of California Press, 2000.

SALDÍVAR-HULL, SONIA, and GENEVA MARIE GANO, eds., *'Ay Tú!': Critical Essays on the Life and Work of Sandra Cisneros*, forthcoming from University of Texas Press, 2024.

HERRERA-SOBEK, MARÍA, and HELENA MARÍA VIRAMONTES, eds., *Chicana Creativity and Criticism: New Frontiers in American Literature*, UNM Press, 1996.

HERRERA-SOBEK, MARÍA, "Social Protest, Folklore, and Feminist Ideology in Chicana Prose and Poetry," *Folklore, Literature, and Cultural Theory*, Routledge, 2014 (pp. 102–116).

REBOLLEDO, TEY DIANA, "Narrative Strategies of Resistance in Hispana Writing," *The Journal of Narrative Technique* 20.2, 1990 (pp. 134–146).

REBOLLEDO, TEY DIANA, and ELIANA S. RIVERA, eds., *Infinite Divisions: An Anthology of Chicana Literature*, University of Arizona Press, 1993.

REBOLLEDO, TEY DIANA, *The Chronicles of Panchita Villa and Other Guerrilleras: Essays on Chicana/Latina Literature and Criticism*, University of Texas Press, 2005.

YARBRO-BEJARANO, YVONÑE, "Mapping Spaces, Marking Time: Transnational Subjectivity, Home, and Family in Stories by Manuel Muñoz and Sandra Cisneros," *Chicana/Latina Studies*, 2013 (pp. 38–64).

BRADY, MARY PAT, *Extinct Lands, Temporal Geographies: Chicana Literature and the Urgency of Space*, Duke University Press, 2002.

BRADY, MARY PAT, "The Contrapuntal Geographies of *Woman Hollering Creek and Other Stories*," *American Literature* 71.1, 1999 (pp. 117–150).

JOHN PHILLIP SANTOS is a poet, journalist, filmmaker, and author, from the Texas–Mexico borderlands. His memoir, *Places Left Unfinished at the Time of Creation*, was a finalist for the National Book Award.

C H R O N O L O G Y

DATE	AUTHOR'S LIFE	LITERARY CONTEXT
1953		Brooks: *Maud Martha*. Tate Gallery exhibit of Mexican painting features multiple artists, including Frida Kahlo.
1954	Born December 20 at 6:47 am at Presbyterian Hospital in Chicago to upholsterer Alfredo Cisneros Del Moral and Elvira Cordero Anguiano. She is the third child following two brothers. Family lives at 3847 W. Grenshaw Street with maternal grandparents, then on South Ashland Avenue between 51st and 53rd Streets, and on W. 63rd Street, 1400 block.	Transtromer: *17 Poems*.
1955		Nabokov: *Lolita*.
1957	Sister Carolina born February 4, dies December 16 of pneumonia. Trip to Mexico to paternal grandparents' home. One other trip to Mexico City pre-1960, father and daughter travel alone by plane.	Bradbury: *Dandelion Wine*. Cheever: *The Wapshot Chronicle*. Kerouac: *On the Road*. Nabokov: *Pnin*. Rand: *Atlas Shrugged*. West: *The Fountain Overflows*. Rosario Castellanos publishes *The Nine Guardians* in Spanish originally.
1958	Brother Carlos born January 24.	*West Side Story* premieres on Broadway.
1959	Brother Arturo born June 25.	José Antonio Villareal publishes *Pocho*, arguably the first Chicano novel. Hansberry: *A Raisin in the Sun*.
1960	Three-car convoy to Mexico with entire family and father's two brothers and their families, a trip that will reappear in *Caramelo*. Twins Mario and Armando born in Mexico City,	Lee: *To Kill a Mockingbird*. O'Brien: *The Country Girls*. Updike: *Rabbit* tetralogy (to 1981).

In Hernandez v. Texas, the Supreme Court acknowledges that Mexican Americans have equal protection under The Fourteenth Amendment. Frida Kahlo dies.

Rosa Parks is arrested and fined for refusing to give her seat on a bus to a white man, leading to the Montgomery Bus Boycott.
Civil Rights Commission established to safeguard voting rights in US. Viet Cong guerrillas attack South Vietnam. EEC founded (Treaty of Rome). USSR launches world's first artificial satellites, Sputnik 1 and 2. First commercial nuclear reactor opens, Pennsylvania. First Frisbees marketed. Ultrasound scanning pioneered in Scotland.

Castro seizes power in Cuba.

J. F. Kennedy elected US President.

DATE	AUTHOR'S LIFE	LITERARY CONTEXT
1960 *cont.*	March 31. Family returns to Chicago, while newborn Mario is left behind in Mexico with paternal grandparents.	
1961	Family returns to Mexico City early in the year to collect infant Mario. Eldest brother Alfred Jr. left behind in Mexico City to be enrolled in military academy for a year to improve his Spanish. Rest of family moves back to Chicago, 4006 W. Gladys Street. Second eldest brother, Henry (Kiki/Quique) takes Sandra to the Chicago Public Library, Legler branch, for her first library card; he teaches her how to walk to school alone without getting lost, tie her shoes, and ride a two-wheel bicycle. Enrolls in public school at Delano Elementary School February, 1st grade because there is no kindergarten, and later Hefferon in September, officially 1st grade.	Heller: *Catch-22*. McCullers: *Clock Without Hands*. Salinger: *Franny and Zooey*.
1962	Attends 2nd grade and part of 3rd grade at St. Mel Holy Ghost (to 1963).	Lessing: *The Golden Notebook*. Nabokov: *Pale Fire*. Rodoreda: *The Time of the Doves*. Spark: *The Prime of Miss Jean Brodie*. Yates: *Eleven Kinds of Loneliness*.
1963	Family moves to 2152 W. Roosevelt Road. Attends St. Calistus, 3rd until mid-6th grade (to 1966). Events occur while in 3rd grade that will be recorded in the story "Eleven."	Friedan: *The Feminine Mystique*. M. McCarthy: *The Group*. Plath: *The Bell Jar*.
1964		Bellow: *Herzog*. Porter: *Collected Stories*.

CHRONOLOGY

Attempted US invasion of Cuba, Bay of Pigs. Berlin Wall erected. Yuri Gagarin first man in space.

Cesar Chavez and Dolores Huertas co-found the National Farm Workers Association (NFWA). Cuban Missile Crisis. First cassette tapes.

Kennedy assassinated; Lyndon Johnson becomes President. Equal Pay Act.

Civil Rights Act outlaws racial discrimination in US. Martin Luther King receives Nobel Peace Prize. Galarza's *Merchants of Labor* exposes abuses within the Bracero program which was supposed to guarantee Mexican seasonal agricultural workers in the US decent living conditions, a minimum wage, shelter and food.
Beatles' first American tour. Leonid Brezhnev ousts Nikita Khrushchev in USSR.

DATE	AUTHOR'S LIFE	LITERARY CONTEXT
1965	Family vacation to Mexico City and Acapulco. Seed for *Caramelo*.	Baldwin: *Going to Meet the Man.* Drabble: *The Millstone.* Mailer: *An American Dream.* Plath: *Ariel.*
1966	Family makes a down-payment on their own home at 1525 N. Campbell St. in the Humboldt Park area, a predominantly Puerto Rican neighborhood on Chicago's North Side. Attends St. Aloysius from mid-6th to 8th grades (graduates in 1968). Teachers are compassionate and kind. Begins writing poetry and fiction.	Rhys: *Wide Sargasso Sea.* Sexton: *Live or Die.*
1967	Father quits working for an interior decorating firm in Winnetka and ventures into his own upholstery business. Unsteady income for several years.	Gonzalez: "I am Joaquin." Márquez: *One Hundred Years of Solitude.* Quinto Sol publishing house is established at UC Berkeley by Octavio L. Romano with Nick C. Vaca and Andres Ybarra and publishes *El Grito: A Journal of Contemporary Mexican-American Thought.*
1968	Attends Josephinum Academy (to 1972), a small Catholic all-girls high school where she writes poetry and is the editor for *NOW*, the school's literary magazine.	Barthelme: *Unspeakable Practices, Unnatural Acts.* Didion: *Slouching Towards Bethlehem.* Poniatowska: *La noche de Tiatelolco.*
1969	Summer trip to Mexico City with female cousin, same age, both first time traveling without adults. Man lands on the moon; but more importantly, menses begins and debuts first bra.	Garro: *Recollections of Things to Come.* Oates: *Them.* Sexton: *Love Poems.*

CHRONOLOGY

US bombs North Vietnam. Large-scale anti-Vietnam War demonstrations begin. October 3: Lyndon Johnson signs the sweeping Hart-Celler Act, a piece of immigration reform legislation that stops the quota system begun in 1924 based on nation of origin (previously, 70 percent of immigration slots were allotted to Northern Europeans). Immigrants with families and who are highly skilled are given priority; it has a transformative effect on American citizenry. Malcolm X assassinated. Selma to Montgomery march against Black voter suppression. Voting Rights Act.

Black Panthers founded, Oakland, California. March 17: Cesar Chavez of the NFWA conducts a march with 75 Latino and Filipino farm workers from Delano, California to the state capitol in Sacramento, over 340 miles, to draw attention to the rights of grape growers. That summer the NFWA combines forces with the Filipino Agricultural Workers Organizing Committee to create the United Farm Workers Organizing Committee (UFWOL), renamed United Farm Workers in 1972.

Mao Zedong launches Cultural Revolution in China.

Racial violence in many US cities; Johnson appoints commission to investigate causes. "Summer of Love," Haight-Ashbury, California. Taking their cue from The Black Panthers, and adopting the motto "To Serve, Observe, and Protect," high school students frequenting La Piranha coffee shop in Los Angeles create the Brown Berets, led by David Sanchez and Carlos Montes. By 1969 there are chapters in 28 cities.

Six-Day War between Israel and Arab states. Che Guevara shot dead, Bolivia.

Student protests in US and throughout Europe. March: Thousands of Chicano students organize and walk out of their classrooms to protest conditions in the Los Angeles Unified School District High Schools in what became known as the Chicano Blowouts. Martin Luther King assassinated. Richard Nixon elected US President. At the Democratic National Convention in Chicago, "anti-patriotic" protesters are barred from demonstrating; thousands appear anyway, leading to clashes with the police and hundreds arrested. December 13: The Mexican-American Legal Defense and Education Fund, modeled on the NAACP, is founded in San Antonio with a $2 million grant from the Ford Foundation.

Soviet invasion of Czechoslovakia.

Neil Armstrong first man on moon. US troops begin withdrawal from Vietnam; still, the US Selective Service System conducts two draft lotteries, conscripting men to fight in Vietnam. Woodstock rock festival attended by 400,000 in New York State.

DATE	AUTHOR'S LIFE	LITERARY CONTEXT
1970		Farah: *From a Crooked Rib.* Morrison: *The Bluest Eye.*
1971		Rivera: *y no se lo tragó la tierra,* wins the Premio Quinto Sol. Du Maurier: *Don't Look Now.* M. McCarthy: *Birds of America.* Munro: *Lives of Girls and Women.* O'Connor: *The Complete Stories.*
1972	Graduates high school. Attends Loyola University, Chicago, studying English (to 1976), where some early poetry is published in the literary journal *Cadence.*	Ayana: *Bless Me, Ultima.*
1973	Family sells Campbell Street house and buys a new home at 1754 N. Keeler, Chicago, moving in on August 3.	Pynchon: *Gravity's Rainbow.* Valdez: "Pensamiento Serpentino," a poem drawing on Mayana philosophical concepts.
1974		Heller: *Something Happened.* Jong: *Fear of Flying.* Paley: *Enormous Changes at the Last Minute.* José Luis Ruiz's film about undocumented immigrants in the US: *Unwanted.*
1975		Bellow: *Humboldt's Gift.* Delaney: *Dhalgren.*
1976	BA from Loyola University (English). Enrolls for MFA course in Creative Writing at University of Iowa (to 1978). On a summer visit to Akumal in the Yucatan, a transcendent experience occurs at the seashore, and in September, she is struck by a car in Iowa City while walking across a highway; both combine to mark the beginning of a spiritual awakening.	Carver: *Will You Please Be Quiet, Please?* Kingston: *The Woman Warrior.* *Fem,* the first Latin American feminist magazine, begins publishing, founded by Alaíde Foppa and Margarita García Flores.

CHRONOLOGY

The Chicano Moratorium against the Vietnam War convenes the largest demonstration of Latinos in US history.

US voting age lowered to eighteen. National Chicana Conference held in Houston, TX to examine role of women in the Movement. Disney World theme park opens in Florida.

India and Pakistan border disputes erupt into full-scale war. Greenpeace founded.

Supreme Court in US rules that abortion is legal. In the time since 1968, more than 50 departments of Chicano studies are founded across California universities. April 16: The mayor of Miami leads a successful petition to make Spanish the city's official second language, creating a department of bilingual affairs. Mobile phones first marketed.

Military coup in Chile: General Pinochet comes to power. Yom Kippur War; oil crisis.

Nixon resigns after Watergate scandal; Gerald Ford becomes US President. Congress passes the Equal Education Opportunities Act, offering bilingual education to Hispanic students. Bangladesh famine.

Vietnam War ends. The Voting Rights Act is extended to Hispanic Americans. Bill Gates and Paul Allen found Microsoft.

Jimmy Carter becomes US President. Chairman Mao dies. First Apple computer.

DATE	AUTHOR'S LIFE	LITERARY CONTEXT
1976 *cont.*	Fall. Lives in a rooming house at 115 East Fairchild Street in Iowa City after abandoning graduate student housing. Goes home to Chicago for Thanksgiving, reads at an open mic at the Great American Coffee House on Lincoln Avenue, Friday, November 26, where she meets poet/activist Carlos Cumpián, who will introduce her to the Chicago Latino arts scene.	
1977		Atwood: *Dancing Girls.* Morrison: *Song of Solomon.*
1978	MFA from University of Iowa (Creative Writing). Thesis is a collection of poetry called *My Wicked Wicked Ways.* Begins writing *The House on Mango Street* while living on Fairchild Street and continues while living in a basement apartment on the 600 block of Church Street. Summer. Returns to Chicago. Carlos Cumpián informs her of a job available at Latino Youth Alternative High School, where she teaches Spanish for Spanish Speakers, Remedial Reading and Creative Writing. Also coordinates the school newspaper; compiles *Un Verano*, a journal of student writing, and co-writes grant proposals for the literary arts component of the school (to 1980). (Also serves as Interim Director, March–September 1980.) Leaves father's house and moves to 4832 W. Homer Street and subsequently 1814 N. Paulina Street. Resumes writing *House* and poetry. Fall. Meets Norma Alarcón at a conference at Northern Illinois University.	Cheever: *Collected Stories.* French: *The Women's Room.* Lessing: *Collected Stories.* McEwan: *In Between the Sheets.*

CHRONOLOGY

Elvis Presley dies. *Star Wars, Saturday Night Fever, Annie Hall* premiere.

June 7: Madrial v Quilligan, a federal class-action lawsuit protesting forced or coerced sterilization of ten Mexican-American women leads to bilingual forms, windows of consideration, and an end to welfare benefits being terminated. Hispanic women able to be more informed about their rights. Camp David Agreement signed by Carter, President Sadat of Egypt and Israeli prime minister Menachem Begin. First "test-tube baby," Louise Brown, born in Oldham, England.

DATE	AUTHOR'S LIFE	LITERARY CONTEXT
1979	Invited by Norma Alarcón to read at University of Indiana, Bloomington, along with poet Sandra María Esteves. Artist-in-Residence, Illinois Arts Council. Teaches poetry workshops in schools throughout the state, from elementary to high school (to 1982).	Calvino: *If on a winter's night a traveler.* Carter: *The Bloody Chamber and Other Stories.* Phillips: *Black Tickets.* Valdez: *Zoot Suit*, the first Chicano play on Broadway. Nicholas Kanellos founds Arte Público Press, creating a national forum for Hispanic literature. Third Woman Press, a queer and feminist of color publisher is founded in Bloomington, Indiana by Norma Alarcón.
1980	*Bad Boys* is published (Mango Press Chicano Chapbook Series #8 funded and produced by poets Lorna Dee Cervantes and Gary Soto). Five-hundred copies printed, sells for $1. Under Chicago artist Diana Solis's leadership, a gathering of Latina writers is organized downtown at the Chicago Cultural Center as part of a Chicago women writers conference (September 13). Norma Alarcón attends and proposes creating a literary magazine to unite Latina writers.	Bambara: *The Salt Eaters* Bowen: *Collected Stories.* Robinson: *Housekeeping.* Welty: *Collected Stories.*
1981	Assistant to the Director, Educational Opportunities Program, Loyola University. Recruiter and counselor (to 1982). Featured in the debut issue of Norma Alarcón's *Third Woman* magazine, Indiana University, Bloomington. Diana Solis's photo of Sandra on the cover. Receives the National Endowment of the Arts Creative Writing Fellowship in Poetry.	Carver: *What We Talk About When We Talk About Love.* Cervantes: *Emplumada.* *This Bridge Called My Back*, a feminist anthology edited by Cherríe Moraga and Gloria Anzaldúa, and a testimony to women of color, first published.

HISTORICAL EVENTS

Soviet troops occupy Afghanistan. Carter and Brezhnev sign SALT II. Shah of Iran forced into exile; Ayatollah Khomeini establishes an Islamic state; American embassy siege in Tehran. Margaret Thatcher becomes the UK's first woman prime minister.

Ronald Reagan elected US President. Iran–Iraq War begins (to 1988). Lech Walesa, shipyard worker, leads strikes in Poland.

Sandra Day O'Connor first woman to serve on the US Supreme Court. Maiden voyage of Space Shuttle. IBM Personal Computer launched.

DATE	AUTHOR'S LIFE	LITERARY CONTEXT
1982	Coordinates "City Songs," funded by the Chicago Council on Fine Arts, a 12-week community poetry workshop for adults. Associate Editor for *Third Woman* magazine, Indiana University, Bloomington. Summer. Subleases an apartment at the Fine Arts Work Center, Provincetown, Massachusetts, with Dennis Mathis, who is helping to edit *The House on Mango Street*. Fall. Leaves for Greece where she lives in Hydra until November 30 and finishes *The House on Mango Street*. Travels through Italy to Paris.	Allende: *The House of the Spirits.* Lorde: *Zami: A New Spelling of My Name.* Márquez: *Chronicle of a Death Foretold.* Tyler: *Dinner in the Homesick Restaurant.* Walker: *The Color Purple.*
1983	Fellow at the Foundation Michael Karolyi in Vence, France, through end of April. Heads back to Greece but is waylaid in Yugoslavia, first on the coast on an island named Rab, May 1, and later that month ventures inland to Sarajevo where she meets Jasna Karaula. While hiking with friends on Trebević mountain, a second spontaneous spiritual experience occurs. Returns to Hydra briefly before flying home to the States in September. Lives outside Chicago at 43W612 Tree Oaks Terrace, Elburn, Illinois, as nanny to a niece. Makes the conscious decision to birth books instead of children. Galeria Quique created, a monthly gathering of writers, painters, and musicians hosted at brother Kiki's loft in Printers Row, Chicago (December 1983 to August 1984).	Carver: *Cathedral.* Mason: *Shiloh and Other Stories.* Moraga: *Loving in the War Years.*

CHRONOLOGY

Beginning of 1980s stock market boom in US. War between UK and Argentina over Falkland Islands.

US troops invade Grenada after government overthrown. CDs launched.

DATE	AUTHOR'S LIFE	LITERARY CONTEXT
1984	In January, *The House on Mango Street* is published (Arte Público Press, Houston). Moves to San Antonio, renting a garage apartment at 630 Mission Street, just beyond the historic King William area. Frustrated and alienated by San Antonio, she invites allies Norma Alarcón and Raul Niño to share her garage apartment for the summer. Literature director at Guadalupe Cultural Arts Center, San Antonio (to 1985). Coordinates monthly reading series with local and guest writers; teaches three creative writing workshops to children, teens, and adults; supervises a poetry-in-the-schools pilot program; interviews guest writers; writes articles for the Center's literary/arts journal, *Tonzantzin*; coordinates the first annual Texas Small Press Book Fair.	Erdrich: *Love Medicine.*
1985	January. Creative Writing Instructor, Texas Lutheran College, Seguin, Texas. Teaches a three-week creative writing workshop during the winter–spring interim session. Receives an Illinois Artists Grant which allows her to finish *My Wicked Wicked Ways* and travel with Norma Alarcón to Mexico in the summer, where she meets Elena Poniatowska. Awarded the Texas Institute of Letters' Dobie-Paisano Fellowship. The fellowship, a residency, delays her planned exit from Texas. She invites writer Ted Dvoracek and Mexican painter José Antonio Aguirre to share the Paisano house with her.	Galeano: *Memories of Fire Trilogy.* Delillo: *White Noise.* Mason: *In Country.* Tyler: *The Accidental Tourist.*

CHRONOLOGY

Reagan re-elected in landslide. Indian prime minister Indira Gandhi assassinated. Famine in Ethiopia.

Reform begins in USSR under new General Secretary of the Communist Party, Mikhail Gorbachev.

DATE	AUTHOR'S LIFE	LITERARY CONTEXT
1985 cont.	*The House on Mango Street* wins the Before Columbus Foundation's American Book Award.	
1986	Receives first and third prizes for the Second Annual Chicano Short Story Award from the University of Arizona. Artist-in-the-Schools, San Antonio Independent School District. Teaches poetry to grades 2 through 5. Rents a house at 838 E. Magnolia Street. Returns to her eldest brother's house in Elburn, Illinois, to write.	Atwood: *The Handmaid's Tale.* Davis: *Break It Down.* Munro: *The Progress of Love.*
1987	Norma Alarcón publishes *My Wicked Wicked Ways* (Third Woman Press, Bloomington, Indiana). Returns to Texas, to share a garage apartment, 1618 W. 12th Street, Austin, with boyfriend Rubén Guzman, who supports her for eight months. Jasna Karaula comes to visit June/July. Initiates a writing workshop at the Women's Peace Center for a few weeks. Experiences a severe depression dubbed "The Year of My Near Death" that ends in December with notification of an NEA Fellowship. Guest professor, California State University, Chico (to 1988). Moves to Chico with Rubén. Rents a furnished faculty member's house at 824 W. Karen Drive, Chico CA for first five months. Second semester moves to 1020 Macy Avenue renting from another faculty member. Teaches three courses including two beginning creative writing classes and one intermediate level fiction writing course.	Gurnah: *Memory of Departure.* Morrison: *Beloved.* Wolfe: *The Bonfire of the Vanities.*

CHRONOLOGY

HISTORICAL EVENTS

US bombs Libya. Gorbachev–Reagan summit. Nuclear explosion in Chernobyl, USSR. Space Shuttle Challenger explodes. Ronald Reagan signs the Immigration Reform and Control Act, giving 2.7 million immigrants permanent legal status, but introduces criminal penalties to employers who knowingly hire workers unauthorized to work in the US.

Reagan makes Berlin Wall speech. World population reaches 5 billion.

DATE	AUTHOR'S LIFE	LITERARY CONTEXT
1988	Susan Bergholz becomes her literary agent. Summer. Returns to Austin and house-sits for friends at 1614 W. 11th Street. Writes poetry for *Loose Woman*, manuscript-in-progress. Fall. Awarded visiting Roberta Holloway Lectureship at the University of California, Berkeley. Teaches a creative writing workshop. Lives at 2275 Virginia Street in Berkeley. Dismayed by her Berkeley students, she visualizes creating an alternative writing workshop with writers working for social change. Jasna Karaula comes to visit October–December.	Allison: *Trash*. Atwood: *Cat's Eye*. Tyler: *Breathing Lessons*.
1989	Moves to a small two-room apartment, 323 W. Adams Street, San Antonio, Texas, number 3, first floor rear, in the King William neighborhood. Works on writing short stories for *Woman Hollering Creek* and an aborted short story that will become *Caramelo*. Second edition of *The House on Mango Street* is published (Vintage Books). Jasna Karaula arrives for an extended US stay, September 1989–May 1990, residing in Elburn, Illinois, with Alfred Cisneros, Jr. and family. *Emergency Tacos: Seven Poets con picante*, a Chicago anthology including Beatriz Badikian, Sandra Cisneros, Carlos Cumpián, Cynthia Gallaher, Margarita Lopez-Castro, Raul Niño, published by March/Abrazo Press, with Carlos Cortez's artwork on cover. One thousand copies printed, sells for $5.	Chávez: *The Face of an Angel*. Hijuelos: *The Mambo Kings Play Songs of Love*. Smiley: *Ordinary Love and Good Will*. Tan: *The Joy Luck Club*.

CHRONOLOGY

George H. W. Bush elected US President. Soviet troops withdrawn in large numbers from Afghanistan. Dr. Lauro Cavazos becomes Secretary of Education, and the first Hispanic member of cabinet.

Berlin Wall dismantled, Communism collapses in Eastern Europe. USSR holds first democratic elections. Tiananmen Square massacre in China. US troops invade Panama. Mexico accounts for 37.1% of immigrants to the US. Tim Berners Lee invents the World Wide Web.

DATE	AUTHOR'S LIFE	LITERARY CONTEXT
1990	Guest professor for one quarter at University of California, Irvine. Teaches "Chicana Writers," and "Rediscovering the Short Story." Lives on campus in a faculty housing complex. Returns to 323 W. Adams Street, in San Antonio, but moves to a one-bedroom apartment across the hall. June–September, Jasna Karaula is her summer guest. Fall. Guest professor at University of Michigan, Ann Arbor, American Studies Department. Teaches "Gender and Literature/Otro modo de ser/Another Way To Be: Latinas in the US" and "Poor Excuses to Get Us Writing: a creative writing workshop." Completes *Woman Hollering Creek* at 400 Maynard Street, Apartment 403. Finishes "Eyes of Zapata." With her students, installs a Day of the Dead altar in the American Studies office, the first created on campus, and meets colleague Ruth Behar at the installation. American Studies Department offers a tenured position, but she turns it down.	Byatt: *Possession*. Espada: *Rebellion is the Circle of a Lover's Hands*. Pritchett: *Complete Short Stories*. Octavio Paz wins the Nobel Prize.
1991	*Woman Hollering Creek* (Random House) is published. *Woman Hollering Creek* is awarded the PEN Center West Award for Best Fiction of 1991, the Quality Paperback Book Club New Voices Award, the Anisfield-Wolf Book Award and the Lannan Foundation Literary Award. It is selected as a noteworthy book of the year by The New York Times and The American Library Journal and nominated Best Book of Fiction for 1991 by The Los Angeles Times.	Alvarez: *How the García Girls Lost their Accents*. Smiley: *A Thousand Acres*.

CHRONOLOGY

DATE	AUTHOR'S LIFE	LITERARY CONTEXT
1991 *cont.*	Guest professor at University of New Mexico, Albuquerque. Leads creative writing workshop, "Poems Tossed Under the Bed." When semester is over, returns to the King William neighborhood in San Antonio and rents an apartment at 309 Madison, second floor rear behind the apartment of Danny López Lozano and Craig Pennel, art influencers.	
1992	June. Third return to Hydra to write the introduction poem for the hardback issue of *My Wicked Wicked Ways*. September. Purchases her first home, a Victorian cottage at 735 E. Guenther Street in the King William area. November. Turtle Bay Books publishes the first hardback edition of *My Wicked Wicked Ways* while Third Woman Press continues publishing the paperback version.	C. McCarthy: *All the Pretty Horses*. Tartt: *The Secret History*. Trevor: *Collected Stories*.
1993	March 7, delivers speech about Jasna Karaula and the Bosnian War for an International Women's Day rally at Travis Park in downtown San Antonio. The speech is published in *The New York Times* in its op-ed pages a week later (March 14), and aired on National Public Radio the following spring along with a letter Jasna later wrote from war-torn Sarajevo. Receives an honorary Doctor of Letters from the State University of New York at Purchase.	Alfaro: *Bitter Homes and Gardens*. Ng: *Bone*. Proulx: *The Shipping News*. Rodriguez: *Always Running: La Vida Loca, Gang Days in LA*. Shields: *The Stone Diaries*.
1994	*Loose Woman* (Knopf) is published. *Hairs/Pelitos* (Knopf) is published. First Vintage Español edition of *La casa en*	Danticat: *Breath, Eyes, Memory*. Heller: *Closing Time*.

CHRONOLOGY

Bill Clinton elected US President. Riots in Los Angeles. Peace agreements lead to end of war in El Salvador.

Palestinian leader Yasser Arafat signs peace agreement with Israeli prime minister Yitzhak Rabin. Janet Reno first woman Attorney General of the US.

The North American Free Trade Agreement (NAFTA) is signed between US, Canada and Mexico, creating a free zone and lifting tariffs on most goods between nations. Mandela's ANC takes power after South African elections. Civil war in Rwanda. Russia takes military action in Chechen

DATE	AUTHOR'S LIFE	LITERARY CONTEXT
1994 *cont.*	*Mango Street*, translated by Elena Poniatowska.	
1995	Receives the MacArthur Foundation Fellowship. Volunteers to teach a summer writing workshop for the Guadalupe Cultural Arts Center. This workshop will evolve into the Macondo Writers' Workshop for socially-engaged writers. First workshop is held at Our Lady of the Lake University.	Nabokov: *Collected Stories*. Smiley: *Moo*. Viramontes: *Under the Feet of Jesus*.
1996	Continues teaching and managing Macondo Writers' Workshop but does so independently. Workshop gathers in her home first few years, eventually moving to several host universities across San Antonio to expand to more than one workshop (to 2013). Writer John Phillip Santos is the first guest teacher.	Atwood: *Alias Grace*. Danticat: *Krik? Krak!* Dubus: *Dancing After Hours*. Gallant: *Collected Stories*. Jen: *Mona in the Promised Land*.
1997	Jasna visits San Antonio briefly. Father dies February 8. Founds the Latino MacArthur Fellows – Los MacArturos – focusing on community outreach; their first reunion in San Antonio, Texas. Becomes embroiled in a legal battle with the San Antonio Historic and Design Review Commission over her decision to paint her Guenther Street home periwinkle (to 1998).	Bolaño: *Last Evenings on Earth*. Roth: *American Pastoral*.
1998	First visit back to Sarajevo after the war. Travels to Croatia with Jasna and visits shrine at Medugorje. European book tour. On return to States, receives The Three Jewels and Five Mindfulness Trainings and the	DeLillo: *Underworld*. Morrison: *Paradise*. Munro: *The Love of a Good Woman*.

CHRONOLOGY

Republic. November 8: Proposition 187 passes in California requiring all health care professionals, teachers and law enforcement officers to report the status of all individuals they deal with to "prevent illegal aliens in the United States from receiving benefits of public services." By 1998, legal challenges render many parts of the proposition unconstitutional.
Oklahoma City bombing. Tejana performer and singer Selena is murdered in Corpus Christi, TX. Rabin assassinated in Israel. Launch of Ebay.

Clinton re-elected US President. Dolly the sheep successfully cloned in Scotland.

Hong Kong sovereignty given back to China by Britain. Economic crisis: stock markets around the world crash, Dow Jones Industrial Average plummets. Madeleine Albright first woman Secretary of State in US. Death of Princess Diana in Paris. Wi-Fi invented.

Clinton impeached over sex scandal (acquitted 1999).

DATE	AUTHOR'S LIFE	LITERARY CONTEXT
1998 *cont.*	Dharma name "Ancestral Home of the Heart" from Thich Nhat Hanh at the Omega Institute, Rhinebeck, New York.	
1999		Lahiri: *Interpreter of Maladies.* Rivera Garza: *Nadie me vera llorar.* Proulx: *Close Range: Wyoming Stories.* Sontag: *In America.*
2000	Founds the Alfredo Cisneros Del Moral Foundation, a grant-giving institution serving Texas writers.	Atwood: *The Blind Assassin.* Kingsolver: *Prodigal Summer.* Oates: *Blonde.*
2001	Finishes *Caramelo* at 730 Canyon Road, Santa Fe, NM, in the adobe home of Juan Ríos on December 12, Virgen de Guadalupe Day.	Franzen: *The Corrections.* Russo: *Empire Falls.*
2002	*Caramelo* (Knopf) is published. Receives an honorary Doctor of Humane Letters from Loyola University, Chicago.	Eugenides: *Middlesex.*
2003	January. Travels to Venice to celebrate completion of *Caramelo*. Jasna joins her. March. Receives the Texas Medal of Arts in Austin and instead of an acceptance speech shares an open letter to First Lady Laura Bush protesting the Iraqi war.	Morrison: *Love.*
2004	*Vintage Cisneros* is published. Jasna comes to visit her brother who has relocated to Atlanta with his family, refugees from the war. Sandra arrives to visit, and they travel from Atlanta together to White Sands, New Mexico.	Danticat: *The Dew Breaker.* Robinson: *Gilead.* Tyler: *The Amateur Marriage.*
2005	*Caramelo* is awarded the Premio Napoli and is short-listed for the Dublin International IMPAC Award. It is also nominated for the Orange Prize in the UK.	Didion: *The Year of Magical Thinking.*

CHRONOLOGY

Ethnic Albanians attacked by Serbs in Kosovo; US leads NATO in bombing of Belgrade.

George W. Bush elected US President. Vladimir Putin succeeds Yeltsin as Russian President. Slobodan Milosevic's regime collapses in former Yugoslavia.

Al-Qaeda attacks New York's World Trade Center; US and allies take action against Taliban in Afghanistan. Wikipedia launched.

Bush declares "War on Terror." Moscow theater hostage crisis.

According to census statistics, Hispanics are the country's largest minority with over 37 million people. Armed, self-appointed militia called minutemen begin patrolling the US southern border and reporting crossings to US border patrol.
US and British troops invade Iraq; Saddam Hussein captured.

Bush re-elected US President. Terrorist bombings in Madrid. Tsunami in Indian Ocean. Facebook launched.

Hurricane Katrina floods New Orleans. Terrorist bombings in London.

DATE	AUTHOR'S LIFE	LITERARY CONTEXT
2006	The Macondo Foundation is officially incorporated with writers Ruth Behar and Richard Blanco as board members.	Eisenberg: *Twilight of the Superheroes.* Santos: *Places Left Unfinished at the Time of Creation.* MacLaverty: *Matters of Life and Death.*
2007	Purchases house across street from her own, Casa Azul, for Macondo. Jasna and sister Zdenka visit San Antonio. Mother dies November 1.	Danticat: *Brother, I'm Dying.* Diaz: *The Brief Wondrous Life of Oscar Wao.*
2008	Paris visit. Jasna joins her. Second San Antonio gathering of Los MacArturos. On October 4, visiting MacArturos gather at the Alamo for a prayer circle of peace and healing, but instead, they are intercepted by the Texas Rangers and almost arrested. Incident is documented by filmmaker Ray Santisteban.	Lahiri: *Unaccustomed Earth.* Robinson: *Home.* Hemon: *The Lazarus Project.*
2009	Invited to install an altar at the National Museum of Mexican Art in Chicago for "Camino a casa: Day of the Dead." First version of altar appears dedicated to her mother: "A Room of Her Own" (September 25–December 13).	Davis: *Collected Stories.* NDiaye: *Three Strong Women.*
2010	Jasna marries. Attends wedding in Sarajevo. Summer. With filmmaker Lourdes Portillo, house-sits UNM professors Tey Diana Rebolledo and Michael Passi's adobe home in Albuquerque. Writes "Canto for Women of a Certain Llanto."	Carson: *Nox.*
2011	*Bravo Bruno!* (La Nuova Frontiera) is published in Italy. Invited to San Miguel de Allende book festival to present *Caramelo.* Installs altar for her mother at the National Hispanic Cultural Center, Albuquerque, New Mexico, with the assistance	Ferrante: *My Brilliant Friend.* Murakami: *IQ84.*

CHRONOLOGY

HISTORICAL EVENTS

Iran joins "nuclear club"; North Korea tests nuclear weapon.

Virginia Tech shooting. Bush reduces US forces in Iraq. Al Gore and UN climate scientists win Nobel Peace Prize. iPhone introduced. Kindle marketed.

Barack Obama, Democratic Senator from Illinois, becomes first Black presidential nominee in US. Collapse of Lehman Brothers triggers world financial crisis.

Ongoing world financial crisis. August 8: Sonia Sotomayor, daughter of Puerto Rican immigrants, raised in the Bronx, is sworn into the US Supreme Court. H1N1 ("swine flu") global pandemic.

Healthcare Reform Bill passed by President Obama. Deepwater Horizon (BP rig) oil spill in Gulf of Mexico. US combat mission ends in Iraq. Ipad introduced.

"Arab Spring": protests and rebellions against repressive regimes across Middle East. Syrian Civil War begins. Osama Bin Laden killed by US Navy Seals.

DATE	AUTHOR'S LIFE	LITERARY CONTEXT
2011 *cont.*	of artist Carolina Rubio. Sells Casa Azul. Reunites with Jasna in Tucson for Jasna's sister's wedding.	
2012	*Have You Seen Marie?* (Knopf) is published. Invited to San Miguel de Allende to introduce Elena Poniatowska at the book festival. Jasna visits States for training in DC in autumn and adds a visit to Sandra in San Antonio.	Munro: *Dear Life.* Smith: *Life on Mars.*
2013	Moves to San Miguel de Allende, Mexico, to finish *A House of My Own*, renting a house on Calle Fuentes, colonia Atascadero.	Adichie: *Americanah.* Messud: *The Woman Upstairs.* Russell: *Vampires in the Lemon Grove.* Saunders: *Tenth of December: Stories.* Tartt: *The Goldfinch.*
2014	Attends short story conference in Vienna, and Jasna joins her. They visit Slovenia afterwards. The Alfredo Cisneros Del Moral Foundation is officially closed. Installs mother's altar at the National Museum of American History (Smithsonian), Washington DC. Sells San Antonio home on December 12.	Kennedy: *All the Rage.* Smiley: *The Last Hundred Years Trilogy* (to 2015).
2015	Completes *A House of My Own: Stories from My Life* on Calle Montitlán in the Balcones area, San Miguel de Allende, published by Knopf. Vintage paperback publication of *My Wicked Wicked Ways.* Buys a house in San Miguel de Allende, summer. After renovations are finished, moves in December 16. The Wittliff Collections at Texas State University acquires Sandra Cisneros's archive. Receives Fifth Star Award presented by the Chicago Department of Cultural Affairs and Special	Lispector: *The Complete Stories.* Morrison: *God Help the Child.* Simpson: *Cockfosters.* Miranda: *Hamilton.* Harjo: *Conflict Resolution for Holy Beings.*

CHRONOLOGY

Obama re-elected US President. Mars Science Laboratory ("Curiosity Rover") lands on Mars. Hurricane Sandy.

Edward Snowden leaks classified documents revealing mass surveillance by the National Security Agency. Boston Marathon bombing. Hispanics make up one-sixth of the US population.

Russia annexes Crimea. ISIS declares Islamic Caliphate.

Black Lives Matter protests begin in US. Supreme Court rules that all states have to recognize same-sex marriage. Islamic terror attacks in Paris. Refugee crisis in Europe.

DATE	AUTHOR'S LIFE	LITERARY CONTEXT
2015 cont.	Events. *The House on Mango Street: Artists Interpret Community*, an art exhibit, featured at the National Museum of Mexican Art, Chicago (April 17–August 23). "Room of Her Own" altar installed at the Museum of Latin American Art, Long Beach, CA.	
2016	Receives the National Medal of Arts from President Barack Obama. Final version of mother's altar featured at the National Museum of Mexican Art in Chicago for "Dia de los Muertos: Journey of the Soul" exhibit (September 23–December 11).	Oyeyemi: *What is Not Yours is Not Yours.*
2017	Jasna undergoes chemotherapy for cancer; Sandra travels to Sarajevo in March and afterwards to Alabama, at the invitation of Billie Jean J. Young, actor/activist/educator. Spiritual experience while visiting the Pettus bridge in Selma. Meets composer Derek Bermel in May. In July at Chautauqua, he presents a suite inspired by *The House on Mango Street*. They begin plans to collaborate on an opera adaptation.	Melchor: *Temporada de hurracanes.*
2018	*Puro Amor* published with illustrations by the author.	Johnson: *The Largesse of the Sea Maiden.*
2019	Receives PEN/Nabokov Award for Achievement in International Literature. Attends Princeton orchestra's performance of Derek Bermel's *Mango Street Suite.*	Evaristo: *Girl, Woman, Other.*
2020	Covid year spent completing *Woman Without Shame* and *Martita* manuscripts.	Diaz: *Postcolonial Love Poem.*

CHRONOLOGY

UK referendum on EU membership results in "Leave" vote. Donald Trump wins US presidential election.

Trump takes up office of President, promising to "make America great again" and fueling rise of populism worldwide. North Korean crisis (to 2018).

US leaves Iran nuclear deal. #MeToo movement goes global.

Protests in Hong Kong. Amazon rainforest wildfires. North Korea nuclear negotiations continue with no agreement. First COVID-19 case in Wuhan, China.

Global COVID-19 pandemic brings life to a halt. George Floyd is murdered by police in Minneapolis, sparking national and international protests. The US Supreme Court, in a 5–4 ruling, thwarts the Trump administration's attempt to put a halt to DACA, the Deferred Action for Childhood Arrivals program, which protected immigrants who came to the US as children from being deported. Donald Trump faces impeachment but is acquitted. Joe Biden elected President.

DATE	AUTHOR'S LIFE	LITERARY CONTEXT
2021	*Martita, I Remember You* published. *The House on Mango Street* chosen for the National Endowment for the Arts Big Read program.	*Postcolonial Love Poem* wins Pulitzer, making Diaz the first Latinx winner in poetry.
2022	May. Meets Jasna in Istanbul. September. *Woman Without Shame* and *Mujer sin vergüenza* are released. Retranslation by Fernanda Melchor of *La casa en Mango Street* (also published in Mexico, where the book is available for the first time). Receives Ruth Lilly Poetry Prize from the Poetry Foundation.	Sánchez: *Crying in the Bathroom: A Memoir.*
2023	February. Travels across North Carolina with poet Reggie Scott Young to visit the homes of writers Carl Sandburg and Betty Smith. April. Visits Betty Smith's home in Brooklyn with Derek Bermel and writer Ruth Behar. June. Receives Mark Twain Award from the Society for the Study of Midwestern Literature. Visits Betty Smith's home in Ann Arbor, Michigan with Ruth Behar. July. Travels to Sarajevo to visit Jasna and to present at the Bookstan Book Fair, the first time she is invited to Sarajevo as an author. Travels to Paris for NYU summer program, a reading at Shakespeare and Company and a craft lecture titled "Over 55 Years Experience, Custom, Quality Work: Notes on Living and Writing." Reunites with Leslie Greene, illustrator of *Bravo Bruno*, and they travel together to Colette's birthplace in Burgundy. August. Presents at La Feria	

CHRONOLOGY

January 6: Violent riots at the US Capitol attempt to disrupt the peaceful transfer of power. US rejoins Paris Climate Accord.

Russia invades Ukraine. Roe v. Wade overturned by Supreme Court; constitutional protection for abortion severed. Inflation rises worldwide. Protesters in Iran march against the country's treatment of women. Pakistan flooding crisis. Death of Queen Elizabeth II. ChatGPT launched.

Turkey–Syria earthquake. 37-count indictment against former president Donald Trump; date of trial set. Ciudad Juárez migrant center fire. Wildfires in Canada. US pandemic-era, "Title 42" (migrant expulsion policy) expires.

DATE	AUTHOR'S LIFE	LITERARY CONTEXT
2023 *cont.*	Internacional del Libro de las Universitarias y de los Universitarias in Mexico City alongside Elena Poniatowska and Liliana Valenzuela. September. Paperback edition of *Woman Without Shame* released. November. Receives The Ambassador Richard C. Holbrooke Distinguished Achievement Award from the Dayton Literary Peace Prize Foundation.	

CHRONOLOGY

The House on Mango Street

CONTENTS

A las Mujeres
To the Women

Introduction: A House of My Own

The young woman in the photograph on the page opposite is me when I was writing *The House on Mango Street*. She's in her office, a room that had probably been a child's bedroom when families lived in this apartment. It has no door and is only slightly wider than the walk-in pantry. But it has great light and sits above the hallway door downstairs, so she can hear her neighbors come and go. She's posed as if she's just looked up from her work for a moment, but in real life she never writes in this office. She writes in the kitchen, the only room with a heater.

It's Chicago, 1980, in the down-at-the-heels Bucktown neighborhood before it's discovered by folks with money. The young woman lives at 1814 N. Paulina Street second floor front. Nelson Algren once wandered these streets. Saul Bellow's turf was over on Division Street, walking distance away. It's a neighborhood that reeks of beer and urine, of sausage and beans.

The young woman fills her "office" with things she drags home from the flea market at Maxwell Street. Antique typewriters, alphabet blocks, asparagus ferns, bookshelves, ceramic figurines from Occupied Japan, wicker baskets, birdcages, hand-painted photos. Things she likes to look at. It's important to have this space to look and think. When she lived at home, the things she looked at scolded her and made her feel sad and depressed. They said, "Wash me." They said, "Lazy." They said, "You ought." But the things in her office are magical and invite her to play. They fill her with light. It's the room where she can be quiet and still and listen to the voices inside herself. She likes being alone in the daytime.

As a girl, she dreamed about having a silent home, just to herself, the way other women dreamed of their weddings. Instead of collecting lace and linen for her trousseau, the young woman buys old things from the thrift stores on grimy Milwaukee Avenue for her future house-of-her-own – faded quilts, cracked vases, chipped saucers, lamps in need of love.

The young woman returned to Chicago after graduate school and moved back into her father's house, 1754 N. Keeler, back into her girl's room with its twin bed and floral wallpaper. She was twenty-three and a half. Now she summoned her courage and told her father she wanted to live alone again, like she did when she was away at school. He looked at her with that eye of the rooster before it attacks, but she wasn't alarmed. She'd seen that look before and knew he was harmless. She was his favorite, and it was only a matter of waiting.

The daughter claimed she'd been taught that a writer needs quiet, privacy, and long stretches of solitude to think. The father decided too much college and too many gringo friends had ruined her. In a way he was right. In a way she was right. When she thinks to herself in her father's language, she knows sons and daughters don't leave their parents' house until they marry. When she thinks in English, she knows she should've been on her own since eighteen.

For a time father and daughter reached a truce. She agreed to move into the basement of a building where the oldest of her six brothers and his wife lived, 4832 W. Homer. But after a few months, when the big brother upstairs turned out to be Big Brother, she got on her bicycle and rode through the neighborhood of her high school days until she spotted an apartment with fresh-painted walls and masking tape on the windows. Then she knocked on the storefront downstairs. That's how she convinced the landlord she was his new tenant.

Her father can't understand why she wants to live in a hundred-year-old building with big windows that let in the cold. She knows her apartment is clean, but the hallway is scuffed and scary, though she and the woman upstairs take turns mopping it regularly. The hall needs paint, and there's nothing they can do about that. When the father visits, he climbs up the stairs muttering with disgust. Inside, he looks at her books arranged in milk crates, at the futon on the floor in a bedroom with no door, and whispers, "Hippie," in the same way he looks at boys hanging out in his neighborhood and says, "*Drogas*." When he sees the space heater in the kitchen, the father shakes his head and sighs, "Why did I work so hard to buy a house with a furnace so she could go backwards and live like this?"

When she's alone, she savors her apartment of high ceilings and windows that let in the sky, the new carpeting and walls white as typing paper, the walk-in pantry with empty shelves, her bedroom without a door, her office with its typewriter, and the big front-room windows with their view of a street, rooftops, trees, and the dizzy traffic of the Kennedy Expressway.

Between her building and the brick wall of the next is a tidy, sunken garden. The only people who ever enter the garden are a family who speak like guitars, a family with a

Southern accent. At dusk they appear with a pet monkey in a cage and sit on a green bench and talk and laugh. She spies on them from behind her bedroom curtains and wonders where they got the monkey.

Her father calls every week to say, "*Mija*, when are you coming home?" What does her mother say about all this? She puts her hands on her hips and boasts, "She gets it from me." When the father is in the room, the mother just shrugs and says, "What can I do?" The mother doesn't object. She knows what it is to live a life filled with regrets, and she doesn't want her daughter to live that life too. She always supported the daughter's projects, so long as she went to school. The mother who painted the walls of their Chicago homes the color of flowers; who planted tomatoes and roses in her garden; sang arias; practiced solos on her son's drum set; boogied along with the *Soul Train* dancers; glued travel posters on her kitchen wall with Karo syrup; herded her kids weekly to the library, to public concerts, to museums; wore a button on her lapel that said "Feed the People Not the Pentagon"; who never went beyond the ninth grade. *That* mother. She nudges her daughter and says, "Good lucky you studied."

The father wants his daughter to be a weather girl on television, or to marry and have babies. She doesn't want to be a TV weather girl. Nor does she want to marry and have babies. Not yet. Maybe later, but there are so many other things she must do in her lifetime first. Travel. Learn how to dance the tango. Publish a book. Live in other cities. Win a National Endowment for the Arts award. See the Northern Lights. Jump out of a cake.

She stares at the ceilings and walls of her apartment the way she once stared at the ceilings and walls of the apartments she grew up in, inventing pictures in the cracks in the plaster, inventing stories to go with these pictures. At night, under the circle of light from a cheap metal lamp clamped to the kitchen table, she sits with paper and a pen and pretends she's not afraid. She's trying to live like a writer.

Where she gets these ideas about living like a writer, she has no clue. She hasn't read Virginia Woolf yet. She doesn't know about Rosario Castellanos or Sor Juana Inés de la Cruz. Gloria Anzaldúa and Cherríe Moraga are cutting their own paths through the world somewhere, but she doesn't know about them. She doesn't know anything. She's making things up as she goes.

When the photo of the young woman who was me was snapped, I still called myself a poet, though I'd been writing stories since grammar school. I'd gravitated back to fiction while in the Iowa poetry workshop. Poetry, as it was taught at Iowa, was a house of cards, a tower of ideas, but I can't communicate an idea except through a story.

The woman I am in the photo was working on a series of vignettes, little by little, along with her poetry. I already had a title – *The House on Mango Street*. Fifty pages had been written, but I still didn't think of it as a novel. It was just a jar of buttons, like the mismatched embroidered pillow-cases and monogrammed napkins I tugged from the bins at the Goodwill. I wrote these things and thought of them as "little stories," though I sensed they were connected to each other. I hadn't heard of story cycles yet. I hadn't read Ermilo Abreu Gómez's *Canek*, Elena Poniatowska's *Lilus Kikus*, Gwendolyn Brooks' *Maud Martha*, Nellie Campobello's *My Mother's Hands*. That would come later, when I had more time and solitude to read.

The woman I once was wrote the first three stories of *House* in one weekend at Iowa. But because I wasn't in the fiction workshop, they wouldn't count toward my MFA thesis. I didn't argue; my thesis advisor reminded me too much of my father. I worked on these little stories on the side for comfort when I wasn't writing poetry for credit. I shared them with colleagues like poet Joy Harjo, who was also having a hard time in the poetry workshops, and fiction writer Dennis Mathis, a small-town Illinois native, but whose paperback library was from the world.

Little-little stories were in literary vogue at the time, in the '70s. Dennis told me about the Japanese Nobel Prize winner Kawabata's minimal "palm of the hand" stories. We fried omelets for dinner and read García Márquez and Heinrich Böll stories aloud. We both preferred experimental writers – all men back then except for Grace Paley – rebels like ourselves. Dennis would become a life-long editor, ally, and voice on the phone when either one of us lost heart.

The young woman in the photo is modeling her book-in-progress after *Dream Tigers* by Jorge Luis Borges – a writer she'd read since high school, story fragments that ring like Hans Christian Andersen, or Ovid, or entries from the encyclopedia. She wants to write stories that ignore borders between genres, between written and spoken, between highbrow literature and children's nursery rhymes, between New York and the imaginary village of Macondo, between the U.S. and Mexico. It's true, she wants the writers she admires to respect her work, but she also wants people who don't usually read books to enjoy these stories too. She *doesn't* want to write a book that a reader won't understand and would feel ashamed for not understanding.

She thinks stories are about beauty. Beauty that is there to be admired by anyone, like a herd of clouds grazing over-head. She thinks people who are busy working for a living deserve beautiful little stories, because they don't have much time and are often tired. She has in mind a book that can be opened at any page and will still make sense to the reader who doesn't know what came before or comes after.

She experiments, creating a text that is as succinct and flexible as poetry, snapping sentences into fragments so that the reader pauses, making each sentence serve *her* and not the other way round, abandoning quotation marks to streamline the typography and make the page as simple and readable as possible. So that the sentences are pliant as branches and can be read in more ways than one.

Sometimes the woman I once was goes out on weekends to meet with other writers. Sometimes I invite these friends to come to my apartment to workshop each other's work. We come from Black, white, Latino communities. We are men and we are women. What we have in common is our sense that art should serve our communities. Together we publish an anthology – *Emergency Tacos* – because we finish our collaborations in the early hours before dawn and gather at the same twenty-four-hour *taquería* on Belmont Avenue, like a multicultural version of Hopper's *Nighthawks* painting. The *Emergency Tacos* writers organize monthly arts events at my brother Keek's apartment – Galeria Quique. We do this with no capital except our valuable time. We do this because the world we live in is a house on fire and the people we love are burning.

The young woman in the photograph gets up in the morning to go to the job that pays the rent on her Paulina Street apartment. She teaches at a school in Pilsen, her mother's old neighborhood on Chicago's south side, a Mexican neighborhood where the rent is cheap and too many families live crowded together. Landlords and the city take no responsibility for the rats, trash that isn't collected often enough, porches that collapse, apartments without fire escapes, until a tragedy happens and several people die. Then they hold investigations for a little while, but the problems go on until the next death, the next investigation, the next bout of forgetting.

The young woman works with students who dropped out of high school but have decided to try again for their diplomas. She learns from her students that they have more difficult lives than her storyteller's imagination can invent. Her life has been comfortable and privileged compared to theirs. She never had to worry about feeding her babies before she went to class. She never had a father or boyfriend who beat her at night and left her bruised in the morning. She didn't have to plan an alternative route to avoid gangs in the school hallway. Her parents didn't plead with her to drop out of school so she could help them earn money.

How can art make a difference in the world? This was never asked at Iowa. Should she be teaching these students to write poetry when they need to know how to defend themselves from someone beating them up? Can a memoir by Malcolm X or a novel by García Márquez save them from the daily blows? And what about those who have such learning problems they can't even manage a book by Dr. Seuss, but can weave a spoken story so wondrous, she wants to take notes. Should she give up writing and study something useful like medicine? How can she teach her students to take control of their own destiny? She loves these students. What should she be doing to save their lives?

The young woman's teaching job leads to the next, and now she finds herself a counselor/recruiter at her alma mater, Loyola University on the north side, in Rogers Park. I have health benefits. I don't bring work home anymore. My work day ends at five p.m. Now I have evenings free to do my own work. I feel like a real writer.

At the university I work for a program that no longer exists, the Educational Opportunity Program, that assists "disadvantaged" students. It's in keeping with my philosophy, and I can still help the students from my previous job. But when my most brilliant student is accepted, enrolls, and drops out in her first semester, I collapse on my desk from grief, from exhaustion, and feel like dropping out myself.

I write about my students because I don't know what else to do with their stories. Writing them down allows me to sleep.

On the weekends, if I can sidestep guilt and avoid my father's demands to come home for Sunday dinner, I'm free to stay home and write. I feel like a bad daughter ignoring my father, but I feel worse when I don't write. Either way, I never feel completely happy.

One Saturday the woman at the typewriter accepts an invitation to a literary soiree. But when she arrives, she feels she's made a terrible mistake. All the writers are old men. She has been invited by Leon Forrest, a Black novelist who was trying to be kind and invite more women, more people-of-color, but so far, she's the only woman, and he and she the only coloreds.

She's there because she's the author of a new book of poetry – *Bad Boys* from Mango Press, the literary efforts of Gary Soto and Lorna Dee Cervantes. Her book is four pages long and was bound together on a kitchen table with a stapler and a spoon. Many of the other guests, she soon realizes, have written *real* books, hardbacks from big New York houses, printed in editions of hundreds of thousands on actual presses. Is she really a writer or is she only pretending to be a writer?

The guest of honor is a famous writer who went to the Iowa Workshop several years before she got there. His latest book has just been sold to Hollywood. He speaks and carries himself as if he's the Emperor of Everything.

At the end of the evening, she finds herself searching for a ride home. She came on the bus, and the Emperor offers to give her a lift home. But she's not going home, she's got her heart set on a movie that's showing only tonight. She's afraid of going to the movies alone, and that's why she's decided to go. Because she's afraid.

The famous writer drives a sports car. The seats smell of leather, and the dashboard is lit like an airplane cockpit. Her own car doesn't always start and has a hole in the floor near the accelerator that lets in rain and snow, so she has to wear boots when she drives. The famous writer talks and talks, but she can't hear what he is saying, because her own thoughts are drowning him out like a wind. She doesn't say anything, doesn't have to. She is just young and pretty enough to feed the famous writer's ego by nodding enthusiastically at everything he says until he drops her off in front of the cinema. She hopes the famous writer notices she is going to see *Gentlemen Prefer Blondes* alone. To tell the truth, she feels miserable walking up to the box office by herself, but she forces herself to buy the ticket and go in because she loves this movie.

The theater is packed. It feels to the young woman as if everybody is there with somebody, except her. Finally, the scene where Marilyn sings "Diamonds Are a Girl's Best Friend." The colors are cartoon-wonderful, the set deliciously campy, the lyrics clever, the whole number is pure old-style glamour. Marilyn is sensational. After her song is over, the audience breaks into applause as if this were a live performance, though sad Marilyn has been dead years and years.

The woman who is me goes home proud of having gone to the movies alone. *See? It wasn't that difficult.* But as she bolts the door of her apartment, she bursts into tears. "I don't have diamonds," she sobs, not knowing what she means, except she knows even then it's not about diamonds. Every few weeks, she has a messy crying jag like this that leaves her feeling shipwrecked and awful. It's such a regular occurrence she thinks these storms of depression are as normal as rain.

What is the woman in the photograph afraid of? She's afraid of walking from her parked car to her apartment in the dark. She's afraid of the scuffling sounds in the walls. She's afraid she'll fall in love and get stuck living in Chicago. She's afraid of ghosts, deep water, rodents, night, things that move too fast – cars, airplanes, her life. She's afraid she'll have to move back home again if she isn't brave enough to live alone.

Throughout all this, I am writing stories to go with that title, *The House on Mango Street*. Sometimes I write about people I remember, sometimes I write about people I've just met, often I mix the two together. My students from Pilsen who sat before me when I was teaching, with girls who sat beside me in another classroom a decade before. I pick up parts of Bucktown, like the monkey garden next door, and plop it down in the Humboldt Park block where I lived during my middle and high school years – 1525 N. Campbell Street.

Often all I have is a title with no story – "The Family of Little Feet," – and I have to make the title kick me in the behind to get me going. Or, sometimes all I've got is a first sentence – "You can never have too much sky." One of my Pilsen students said I had said this, and she never forgot it. Good thing she remembered and quoted it back to me. "They came with the wind that blows in August . . ." This line came to me in a dream. Sometimes the best ideas come in dreams. Sometimes the worst ideas come from there, too!

Whether the idea came from a sentence I heard buzzing around somewhere and saved in a jar, or from a title I picked up and pocketed, the stories always insist on telling me where they want to end. They often surprise me by stopping when I had every intention of galloping along a little further. They're stubborn. They know best when there's no more to be said. The last sentence must ring like the final notes at the end of a mariachi song – *tan-tán* – to tell you when the song is done.

The people I wrote about were real, for the most part, from here and there, now and then, but sometimes three real people would be braided together into one made-up person. Usually when I thought I was creating someone from my imagination, it turned out I was remembering someone I'd forgotten or someone standing so close I couldn't see her at all.

I cut apart and stitched together events to tailor the story, gave it shape so it had a beginning, middle, and end, because real life stories rarely come to us complete. Emotions, though, can't be invented, can't be borrowed. All the emotions my characters feel, good or bad, are mine.

I meet Norma Alarcón. She is to become one of my earliest publishers and my lifetime friend. The first time she walks through the rooms of the apartment on North Paulina, she notices the quiet rooms, the collection of typewriters, the books and Japanese figurines, the windows with the view of freeway and sky. She walks as if on tiptoe, peering into every room, even the pantry and closet as if looking for something. "You live here . . ." she asks, "alone?"

"Yes."

"So . . ." She pauses. "How did you do it?"

Norma, I did it by doing the things I was afraid of doing so that I would no longer be afraid. Moving away to go to graduate school. Traveling abroad alone. Earning my own money and living by myself. Posing as an author when I was afraid, just as I posed in that photo you used on the first cover of *Third Woman*.

And, finally, when I was ready, after I had apprenticed with professional writers over several years, partnering with the right agent. My father, who sighed and wished for me to marry, was, at the end of his life, much more gratified I had my agent Susan Bergholz providing for me rather than a husband. *¿Ha llamado Susan?* he asked me daily, because if Susan called it meant good news. Diamonds may do for a girl, but an agent is a woman writer's best friend.

I couldn't trust my own voice, Norma. People saw a little girl when they looked at me and heard a little girl's voice when I spoke. Because I was unsure of my own adult voice and often censored myself, I made up another voice, Esperanza's, to be my voice and ask the things I needed answers to myself – "Which way?" I didn't know exactly, but I knew which routes I didn't want to take – Sally, Rafaela, Ruthie – women whose lives were white crosses on the roadside.

At Iowa we never talked about serving others with our writing. It was all about serving ourselves. But there were no other examples to follow until you introduced me to Mexican writers Sor Juana Inés de la Cruz, Elena Poniatowska, Elena Garro, Rosario Castellanos. The young woman in the photograph was looking for another way to be – "*otro modo de ser*," as Castellanos put it.

Until you brought us all together as U.S. Latina writers – Cherríe Moraga, Gloria Anzaldúa, Marjorie Agosín, Carla Trujillo, Diana Solís, Sandra María Esteves, Diane Gómez, Salima Rivera, Margarita López, Beatriz Badikian, Carmen Abrego, Denise Chávez, Helena Viramontes – until then, Normita, we had no idea what we were doing was extraordinary.

I no longer make Chicago my home, but Chicago still makes its home in me. I have Chicago stories I have yet to write. So long as those stories kick inside me, Chicago will still be home.

Eventually I took a job in San Antonio. Left. Came back. And left again. I kept coming back lured by cheap rent. Affordable housing is essential to an artist. I could, in time, even buy my own first house, a hundred-year-old home once periwinkle, but now painted a Mexican pink.

Two years ago my office went up in my backyard, a building created from my Mexican memories. I am writing this today from this very office, Mexican marigold on the outside, morning-glory violet on the inside. Wind chimes ring from the terrace. Trains moan in the distance all the time, ours is a neighborhood of trains. The same San Antonio River tourists know from the Riverwalk wends its way behind my house to the Missions and beyond until it empties into the Gulf of Mexico. From my terrace you can see the river where it bends into an S.

White cranes float across the sky like a scene painted on a lacquered screen. The river shares the land with ducks, raccoons, possums, skunks, buzzards, butterflies, hawks, turtles, snakes, owls, even though we're walking distance to downtown. And within the confines of my own garden there are plenty of other creatures too – yappy dogs, kamikaze cats, one lovesick parrot with a crush on me.

This is my house.

Bliss.

October 24th, 2007. You come down from Chicago for a visit, Mama. You don't want to come. I make you come. You don't like to leave your house anymore, your back hurts you say, but I insist. I built this office beside the river for you as much as for me, and I want you to see it.

Once, years ago, you telephoned and said in an urgent voice, "When are you going to build your office? I just saw Isabel Allende on PBS and she has a HUGE desk and a BIG office." You were upset because I was writing on the kitchen table again like in the old days.

And now here we are, on the rooftop of a saffron building with a river view, a space all my own just to write. We climb up to the room I work in, above the library, and out to the balcony facing the river.

You have to rest. There are industrial buildings on the opposite bank – abandoned granaries and silos – but they're so rain-rusted and sun-bleached, they have their own charm, like public sculptures. When you've recovered your breath, we continue.

I'm especially proud of the spiral staircase to the rooftop. I'd always dreamed of having one, just like the houses in Mexico. Even the word for them in Spanish is wonderful – *un caracol* – a snail. Our footsteps clang on each metal step, the dogs following so close we have to scold them.

"Your office is bigger than in the pictures you sent," you say delighted. I imagine you're comparing it to Isabel Allende's.

"Where did you get the drapes in the library? I bet they cost a pretty penny. Too bad your brothers couldn't upholster your chairs for you and save you some money. Boy, this place is niiiiice!" you say, your voice sliding up the scales like a river grackle.

I plop yoga mats on the rooftop, and we sit cross-legged to watch the sun descend. We drink your favorite, Italian sparkling wine, to celebrate your arrival, to celebrate my office.

The sky absorbs the night quickly-quickly, dissolving into the color of a plum. I lie on my back and watch clouds scurry past in a hurry to get home. Stars come out shyly, one by one. You lie down next to me and drape one leg over mine like when we sleep together at your home. We always sleep together when I'm there. At first because there isn't any other bed. But later, after Papa dies, just because you want me near. It's the only time you let yourself be affectionate.

"What if we invite everybody down here for Christmas next year?" I ask, "What do you think?"

"We'll see," you say lost in your own thoughts.

The moon climbs the front yard mesquite tree, leaps over the terrace ledge and astonishes us. It's a full moon, a huge nimbus like the prints of Yoshitoshi. From here on, I won't be able to see a full moon again without thinking of you, this moment. But right now, I don't know this.

You close your eyes. You look like you're sleeping. The

plane ride must've tired you. "Good lucky you studied," you
say without opening your eyes. You mean my office, my life.
I say to you, "Good lucky."

For my mother, Elvira Cordero Cisneros
July 11th, 1929–November 1st, 2007

May 26th, 2008
Casa Xóchitl, San Antonio de Béxar, Texas

THE HOUSE ON
MANGO STREET

The House on Mango Street

We didn't always live on Mango Street. Before that we lived on Loomis on the third floor, and before that we lived on Keeler. Before Keeler it was Paulina, and before that I can't remember. But what I remember most is moving a lot. Each time it seemed there'd be one more of us. By the time we got to Mango Street we were six – Mama, Papa, Carlos, Kiki, my sister Nenny and me.

The house on Mango Street is ours, and we don't have to pay rent to anybody, or share the yard with the people downstairs, or be careful not to make too much noise, and there isn't a landlord banging on the ceiling with a broom. But even so, it's not the house we'd thought we'd get.

We had to leave the flat on Loomis quick. The water pipes broke and the landlord wouldn't fix them because the house was too old. We had to leave fast. We were using the washroom next door and carrying water over in empty milk gallons. That's why Mama and Papa looked for a house, and that's why we moved into the house on Mango Street, far away, on the other side of town.

They always told us that one day we would move into
a house, a real house that would be ours for always so we
wouldn't have to move each year. And our house would have
running water and pipes that worked. And inside it would
have real stairs, not hallway stairs, but stairs inside like the
houses on T.V. And we'd have a basement and at least three
washrooms so when we took a bath we wouldn't have to tell
everybody. Our house would be white with trees around it,
a great big yard and grass growing without a fence. This was
the house Papa talked about when he held a lottery ticket and
this was the house Mama dreamed up in the stories she told
us before we went to bed.

But the house on Mango Street is not the way they told it
at all. It's small and red with tight steps in front and windows
so small you'd think they were holding their breath. Bricks
are crumbling in places, and the front door is so swollen you
have to push hard to get in. There is no front yard, only
four little elms the city planted by the curb. Out back is a
small garage for the car we don't own yet and a small yard
that looks smaller between the two buildings on either side.
There are stairs in our house, but they're ordinary hallway
stairs, and the house has only one washroom. Everybody has
to share a bedroom – Mama and Papa, Carlos and Kiki, me
and Nenny.

Once when we were living on Loomis, a nun from my
school passed by and saw me playing out front. The laundromat downstairs had been boarded up because it had been
robbed two days before and the owner had painted on the
wood YES WE'RE OPEN so as not to lose business.

Where do you live? she asked.

There, I said pointing up to the third floor.

You live *there?*

There. I had to look to where she pointed – the third
floor, the paint peeling, wooden bars Papa had nailed on the
windows so we wouldn't fall out. You live *there?* The way

she said it made me feel like nothing. *There.* I lived *there.* I nodded.

I knew then I had to have a house. A real house. One I could point to. But this isn't it. The house on Mango Street isn't it. For the time being, Mama says. Temporary, says Papa. But I know how those things go.

Hairs

Everybody in our family has different hair. My Papa's hair is like a broom, all up in the air. And me, my hair is lazy. It never obeys barrettes or bands. Carlos' hair is thick and straight. He doesn't need to comb it. Nenny's hair is slippery – slides out of your hand. And Kiki, who is the youngest, has hair like fur.

But my mother's hair, my mother's hair, like little rosettes, like little candy circles all curly and pretty because she pinned it in pincurls all day, sweet to put your nose into when she is holding you, holding you and you feel safe, is the warm smell of bread before you bake it, is the smell when she makes room for you on her side of the bed still warm with her skin, and you sleep near her, the rain outside falling and Papa snoring. The snoring, the rain, and Mama's hair that smells like bread.

Boys & Girls

The boys and the girls live in separate worlds. The boys in their universe and we in ours. My brothers for example. They've got plenty to say to me and Nenny inside the house. But outside they can't be seen talking to girls. Carlos and Kiki are each other's best friend . . . not ours.

Nenny is too young to be my friend. She's just my sister and that was not my fault. You don't pick your sisters, you just get them and sometimes they come like Nenny.

She can't play with those Vargas kids or she'll turn out just like them. And since she comes right after me, she is my responsibility.

Someday I will have a best friend all my own. One I can tell my secrets to. One who will understand my jokes without my having to explain them. Until then I am a red balloon, a balloon tied to an anchor.

My Name

In English my name means hope. In Spanish it means too many letters. It means sadness, it means waiting. It is like the number nine. A muddy color. It is the Mexican records my father plays on Sunday mornings when he is shaving, songs like sobbing.

It was my great-grandmother's name and now it is mine. She was a horse woman too, born like me in the Chinese year of the horse – which is supposed to be bad luck if you're born female – but I think this is a Chinese lie because the Chinese, like the Mexicans, don't like their women strong.

My great-grandmother. I would've liked to have known her, a wild horse of a woman, so wild she wouldn't marry. Until my great-grandfather threw a sack over her head and carried her off. Just like that, as if she were a fancy chandelier. That's the way he did it.

And the story goes she never forgave him. She looked out the window her whole life, the way so many women sit their sadness on an elbow. I wonder if she made the best with what she got or was she sorry because she couldn't be all the things she wanted to be. Esperanza. I have inherited her name, but I don't want to inherit her place by the window.

At school they say my name funny as if the syllables were made out of tin and hurt the roof of your mouth. But in Spanish my name is made out of a softer something, like silver, not quite as thick as sister's name – Magdalena – which is uglier than mine. Magdalena who at least can come home and become Nenny. But I am always Esperanza.

I would like to baptize myself under a new name, a name more like the real me, the one nobody sees. Esperanza as Lisandra or Maritza or Zeze the X. Yes. Something like Zeze the X will do.

Cathy Queen of Cats

She says, I am the great great grand cousin of the queen of France. She lives upstairs, over there, next door to Joe the baby-grabber. Keep away from him, she says. He is full of danger. Benny and Blanca own the corner store. They're okay except don't lean on the candy counter. Two girls raggedy as rats live across the street. You don't want to know them. Edna is the lady who owns the building next to you. She used to own a building big as a whale, but her brother sold it. Their mother said no, no, don't ever sell it. I won't. And then she closed her eyes and he sold it. Alicia is stuck-up ever since she went to college. She used to like me but now she doesn't.

Cathy who is queen of cats has cats and cats and cats. Baby cats, big cats, skinny cats, sick cats. Cats asleep like little donuts. Cats on top of the refrigerator. Cats taking a walk on the dinner table. Her house is like cat heaven.

You want a friend, she says. Okay, I'll be your friend. But only till next Tuesday. That's when we move away. Got to. Then as if she forgot I just moved in, she says the neighborhood is getting bad.

Cathy's father will have to fly to France one day and find her great great distant grand cousin on her father's side and inherit the family house. How do I know this is so? She told me so. In the meantime they'll just have to move a little farther north from Mango Street, a little farther away every time people like us keep moving in.

Our Good Day

If you give me five dollars I will be your friend forever. That's what the little one tells me.

Five dollars is cheap since I don't have any friends except Cathy who is only my friend till Tuesday.

Five dollars, five dollars.

She is trying to get somebody to chip in so they can buy a bicycle from this kid named Tito. They already have ten dollars and all they need is five more.

Only five dollars, she says.

Don't talk to them, says Cathy. Can't you see they smell like a broom.

But I like them. Their clothes are crooked and old. They are wearing shiny Sunday shoes without socks. It makes their bald ankles all red, but I like them. Especially the big one who laughs with all her teeth. I like her even though she lets the little one do all the talking.

Five dollars, the little one says, only five.

Cathy is tugging my arm and I know whatever I do next will make her mad forever.

Wait a minute, I say, and run inside to get the five dollars. I have three dollars saved and I take two of Nenny's. She's not home, but I'm sure she'll be glad when she finds out we own a bike. When I get back, Cathy is gone like I knew she would be, but I don't care. I have two new friends and a bike too.

My name is Lucy, the big one says. This here is Rachel my sister.

I'm her sister, says Rachel. Who are you?

And I wish my name was Cassandra or Alexis or Maritza – anything but Esperanza – but when I tell them my name they don't laugh.

We come from Texas, Lucy says and grins. Her was born here, but me I'm Texas.

You mean *she*, I say.

No, I'm from Texas, and doesn't get it.

This bike is three ways ours, says Rachel who is thinking ahead already. Mine today, Lucy's tomorrow and yours day after.

But everybody wants to ride it today because the bike is new, so we decide to take turns *after* tomorrow. Today it belongs to all of us.

I don't tell them about Nenny just yet. It's too complicated. Especially since Rachel almost put out Lucy's eye about who was going to get to ride it first. But finally we agree to ride it together. Why not?

Because Lucy has long legs she pedals. I sit on the back seat and Rachel is skinny enough to get up on the handlebars which makes the bike all wobbly as if the wheels are spaghetti, but after a bit you get used to it.

We ride fast and faster. Past my house, sad and red and crumbly in places, past Mr. Benny's grocery on the corner, and down the avenue which is dangerous. Laundromat, junk store, drugstore, windows and cars and more cars, and around the block back to Mango.

People on the bus wave. A very fat lady crossing the street says, You sure got quite a load there.

Rachel shouts, You got quite a load there too. She is very sassy.

Down, down Mango Street we go. Rachel, Lucy, me. Our new bicycle. Laughing the crooked ride back.

Laughter

Nenny and I don't look like sisters . . . not right away. Not the way you can tell with Rachel and Lucy who have the same fat popsicle lips like everybody else in their family. But me and Nenny, we are more alike than you would know. Our laughter for example. Not the shy ice cream bells' giggle of Rachel and Lucy's family, but all of a sudden and surprised like a pile of dishes breaking. And other things I can't explain.

One day we were passing a house that looked, in my mind, like houses I had seen in Mexico. I don't know why. There was nothing about the house that looked exactly like the houses I remembered. I'm not even sure why I thought it, but it seemed to feel right.

Look at that house, I said, it looks like Mexico.

Rachel and Lucy look at me like I'm crazy, but before they can let out a laugh, Nenny says: Yes, that's Mexico all right. That's what I was thinking exactly.

Gil's Furniture Bought & Sold

There is a junk store. An old man owns it. We bought a used refrigerator from him once, and Carlos sold a box of magazines for a dollar. The store is small with just a dirty window for light. He doesn't turn the lights on unless you got money to buy things with, so in the dark we look and see all kinds of things, me and Nenny. Tables with their feet upside-down and rows and rows of refrigerators with round corners and couches that spin dust in the air when you punch them and a hundred T.V.'s that don't work probably. Everything is on top of everything so the whole store has skinny aisles to walk through. You can get lost easy.

The owner, he is a black man who doesn't talk much and sometimes if you didn't know better you could be in there a long time before your eyes notice a pair of gold glasses floating in the dark. Nenny who thinks she is smart and talks to any old man, asks lots of questions. Me, I never said nothing to him except once when I bought the Statue of Liberty for a dime.

But Nenny, I hear her asking one time how's this here and

the man says, This, this is a music box, and I turn around quick thinking he means a *pretty* box with flowers painted on it, with a ballerina inside. Only there's nothing like that where this old man is pointing, just a wood box that's old and got a big brass record in it with holes. Then he starts it up and all sorts of things start happening. It's like all of a sudden he let go a million moths all over the dusty furniture and swan-neck shadows and in our bones. It's like drops of water. Or like marimbas only with a funny little plucked sound to it like if you were running your fingers across the teeth of a metal comb.

And then I don't know why, but I have to turn around and pretend I don't care about the box so Nenny won't see how stupid I am. But Nenny, who is stupider, already is asking how much and I can see her fingers going for the quarters in her pants pocket.

This, the old man says shutting the lid, this ain't for sale.

Meme Ortiz

Meme Ortiz moved into Cathy's house after her family moved away. His name isn't really Meme. His name is Juan. But when we asked him what his name was he said Meme, and that's what everybody calls him except his mother.

Meme has a dog with gray eyes, a sheepdog with two names, one in English and one in Spanish. The dog is big, like a man dressed in a dog suit, and runs the same way its owner does, clumsy and wild and with the limbs flopping all over the place like untied shoes.

Cathy's father built the house Meme moved into. It is wooden. Inside the floors slant. Some rooms uphill. Some down. And there are no closets. Out front there are twenty-one steps, all lopsided and jutting like crooked teeth (made that way on purpose, Cathy said, so the rain will slide off), and when Meme's mama calls from the doorway, Meme goes scrambling up the twenty-one wooden stairs with the dog with two names scrambling after him.

Around the back is a yard, mostly dirt, and a greasy bunch of boards that used to be a garage. But what you remember most is this tree, huge, with fat arms and mighty families of squirrels in the higher branches. All around, the neighborhood of roofs, black-tarred and A-framed, and in their gutters, the balls that never came back down to earth. Down at the base of the tree, the dog with two names barks into the empty air, and there at the end of the block, looking smaller still, our house with its feet tucked under like a cat.

This is the tree we chose for the First Annual Tarzan Jumping Contest. Meme won. And broke both arms.

Louie, His Cousin & His Other Cousin

Downstairs from Meme's is a basement apartment that Meme's mother fixed up and rented to a Puerto Rican family. Louie's family. Louie is the oldest in a family of little sisters. He is my brother's friend really, but I know he has two cousins and that his T-shirts never stay tucked in his pants.

Louie's girl cousin is older than us. She lives with Louie's family because her own family is in Puerto Rico. Her name is Marin or Maris or something like that, and she wears dark nylons all the time and lots of makeup she gets free from selling Avon. She can't come out – gotta baby-sit with Louie's sisters – but she stands in the doorway a lot, all the time singing, clicking her fingers, the same song:

> *Apples, peaches, pumpkin pah-ay.*
> *You're in love and so am ah-ay.*

Louie has another cousin. We only saw him once, but it was important. We were playing volleyball in the alley when he drove up in this great big yellow Cadillac with whitewalls and a yellow scarf tied around the mirror. Louie's cousin had his arm out the window. He honked a couple of times and a lot of faces looked out from Louie's back window and then a lot of people came out – Louie, Marin and all the little sisters.

Everybody looked inside the car and asked where he got it. There were white rugs and white leather seats. We all asked for a ride and asked where he got it. Louie's cousin said get in.

We each had to sit with one of Louie's little sisters on our lap, but that was okay. The seats were big and soft like a sofa, and there was a little white cat in the back window whose eyes lit up when the car stopped or turned. The windows didn't roll up like in ordinary cars. Instead there was a button that did it for you automatically. We rode up the alley and around the block six times, but Louie's cousin said he was going to make us walk home if we didn't stop playing with the windows or touching the FM radio.

The seventh time we drove into the alley we heard sirens . . . real quiet at first, but then louder. Louie's cousin stopped the car right where we were and said, Everybody out of the car. Then he took off flooring that car into a yellow blur. We hardly had time to think when the cop car pulled in the alley going just as fast. We saw the yellow Cadillac at the end of the block trying to make a left-hand turn, but our alley is too skinny and the car crashed into a lamppost.

Marin screamed and we ran down the block to where the cop car's siren spun a dizzy blue. The nose of that yellow Cadillac was all pleated like an alligator's, and except for a bloody lip and a bruised forehead, Louie's cousin was okay. They put handcuffs on him and put him in the backseat of the cop car, and we all waved as they drove away.

Marin

Marin's boyfriend is in Puerto Rico. She shows us his letters and makes us promise not to tell anybody they're getting married when she goes back to P.R. She says he didn't get a job yet, but she's saving the money she gets from selling Avon and taking care of her cousins.

Marin says that if she stays here next year, she's going to get a real job downtown because that's where the best jobs are, since you always get to look beautiful and get to wear nice clothes and can meet someone in the subway who might marry you and take you to live in a big house far away.

But next year Louie's parents are going to send her back to her mother with a letter saying she's too much trouble, and that is too bad because I like Marin. She is older and knows lots of things. She is the one who told us how Davey the Baby's sister got pregnant and what cream is best for taking off moustache hair and if you count the white flecks on your fingernails you can know how many boys are thinking of you and lots of other things I can't remember now.

We never see Marin until her aunt comes home from

work, and even then she can only stay out in front. She is there every night with the radio. When the light in her aunt's room goes out, Marin lights a cigarette and it doesn't matter if it's cold out or if the radio doesn't work or if we've got nothing to say to each other. What matters, Marin says, is for the boys to see us and for us to see them. And since Marin's skirts are shorter and since her eyes are pretty, and since Marin is already older than us in many ways, the boys who do pass by say stupid things like I am in love with those two green apples you call eyes, give them to me why don't you. And Marin just looks at them without even blinking and is not afraid.

Marin, under the streetlight, dancing by herself, is singing the same song somewhere. I know. Is waiting for a car to stop, a star to fall, someone to change her life.

Those Who Don't

Those who don't know any better come into our neighbor-hood scared. They think we're dangerous. They think we will attack them with shiny knives. They are stupid people who are lost and got here by mistake.

But we aren't afraid. We know the guy with the crooked eye is Davey the Baby's brother, and the tall one next to him in the straw brim, that's Rosa's Eddie V., and the big one that looks like a dumb grown man, he's Fat Boy, though he's not fat anymore nor a boy.

All brown all around, we are safe. But watch us drive into a neighborhood of another color and our knees go shakity-shake and our car windows get rolled up tight and our eyes look straight. Yeah. That is how it goes and goes.

There Was an Old Woman She Had So Many Children She Didn't Know What to Do

Rosa Vargas' kids are too many and too much. It's not her fault you know, except she is their mother and only one against so many.

They are bad those Vargases, and how can they help it with only one mother who is tired all the time from button-ing and bottling and babying, and who cries every day for the man who left without even leaving a dollar for bologna or a note explaining how come.

The kids bend trees and bounce between cars and dangle upside-down from knees and almost break like fancy museum vases you can't replace. They think it's funny. They are with-out respect for all things living, including themselves.

But after a while you get tired of being worried about kids who aren't even yours. One day they are playing chicken on Mr. Benny's roof. Mr. Benny says, Hey ain't you kids know better than to be swinging up there? Come down, you come down right now, and then they just spit.

See. That's what I mean. No wonder everybody gave up. Just stopped looking out when little Efren chipped his buck tooth on a parking meter and didn't even stop Refugia from getting her head stuck between two slats in the back gate and nobody looked up not once the day Angel Vargas learned to fly and dropped from the sky like a sugar donut, just like a falling star, and exploded down to earth without even an "Oh."

Alicia Who Sees Mice

Close your eyes and they'll go away, her father says, or You're just imagining. And anyway, a woman's place is sleeping so she can wake up early with the tortilla star, the one that appears early just in time to rise and catch the hind legs hide behind the sink, beneath the four-clawed tub, under the swollen floorboards nobody fixes, in the corner of your eyes.

Alicia, whose mama died, is sorry there is no one older to rise and make the lunchbox tortillas. Alicia, who inherited her mama's rolling pin and sleepiness, is young and smart and studies for the first time at the university. Two trains and a bus, because she doesn't want to spend her whole life in a factory or behind a rolling pin. Is a good girl, my friend, studies all night and sees the mice, the ones her father says do not exist. Is afraid of nothing except four-legged fur. And fathers.

Darius & the Clouds

You can never have too much sky. You can fall asleep and wake up drunk on sky, and sky can keep you safe when you are sad. Here there is too much sadness and not enough sky. Butterflies too are few and so are flowers and most things that are beautiful. Still, we take what we can get and make the best of it.

Darius, who doesn't like school, who is sometimes stupid and mostly a fool, said something wise today, though most days he says nothing. Darius, who chases girls with firecrackers or a stick that touched a rat and thinks he's tough, today pointed up because the world was full of clouds, the kind like pillows.

You all see that cloud, that fat one there? Darius said, See that? Where? That one next to the one that look like popcorn. That one there. See that. That's God, Darius said. God? somebody little asked. God, he said, and made it simple.

And Some More

The Eskimos got thirty different names for snow, I say. I read it in a book.

I got a cousin, Rachel says. She got three different names.

There ain't thirty different kinds of snow, Lucy says. There are two kinds. The clean kind and the dirty kind, clean and dirty. Only two.

There are a million zillion kinds, says Nenny. No two exactly alike. Only how do you remember which one is which?

She got three last names and, let me see, two first names. One in English and one in Spanish . . .

And clouds got at least ten different names, I say.

Names for clouds? Nenny asks. Names just like you and me?

That up there, that's cumulus, and everybody looks up.

Cumulus are cute, Rachel says. She *would* say something like that.

What's that one there? Nenny asks, pointing a finger.

That's cumulus too. They're all cumulus today. Cumulus, cumulus, cumulus.

No, she says. That there is Nancy, otherwise known as Pig-eye. And over there her cousin Mildred, and little Joey, Marco, Nereida and Sue.

There are all different kinds of clouds. How many different kinds of clouds can you think of?

Well, there's these already that look like shaving cream . . .

And what about the kind that looks like you combed its hair? Yes, those are clouds too.

Phyllis, Ted, Alfredo and Julie . . .

There are clouds that look like big fields of sheep, Rachel says. Them are my favorite.

And don't forget nimbus the rain cloud, I add, that's something.

Jose and Dagoberto, Alicia, Raul, Edna, Alma and Rickey . . .

There's that wide puffy cloud that looks like your face when you wake up after falling asleep with all your clothes on.

Reynaldo, Angelo, Albert, Armando, Mario . . .

Not my face. Looks like your fat face.

Rita, Margie, Ernie . . .

Whose fat face?

Esperanza's fat face, that's who. Looks like Esperanza's ugly face when she comes to school in the morning.

Anita, Stella, Dennis, and Lolo . . .

Who you calling ugly, ugly?

Richie, Yolanda, Hector, Stevie, Vincent . . .

Not you. Your mama, that's who.

My mama? You better not be saying that, Lucy Guerrero. You better not be talking like that . . . else you can say good-bye to being my friend forever.

I'm saying your mama's ugly like . . . ummm . . .

. . . like bare feet in September!

That does it! Both of yous better get out of my yard before I call my brothers.

Oh, we're only playing.

I can think of thirty Eskimo words for you, Rachel. Thirty words that say what you are.

Oh yeah, well I can think of some more.

Uh-oh, Nenny. Better get the broom. Too much trash in our yard today.

Frankie, Licha, Maria, Pee Wee . . .

Nenny, you better tell your sister she is really crazy because Lucy and me are never coming back here again. Forever.

Reggie, Elizabeth, Lisa, Louie . . .

You can do what you want to do, Nenny, but you better not talk to Lucy or Rachel if you want to be my sister.

You know what you are, Esperanza? You are like the Cream of Wheat cereal. You're like the lumps.

Yeah, and you're foot fleas, that's you.

Chicken lips.

Rosemary, Dalia, Lily . . .

Cockroach jelly.

Jean, Geranium and Joe . . .

Cold *frijoles*.

Mimi, Michael, Moe . . .

Your mama's *frijoles*.

Your ugly mama's toes.

That's stupid.

Bebe, Blanca, Benny . . .

Who's stupid?

Rachel, Lucy, Esperanza, and Nenny.

The Family of Little Feet

There was a family. All were little. Their arms were little, and their hands were little, and their height was not tall, and their feet very small.

The grandpa slept on the living room couch and snored through his teeth. His feet were fat and doughy like thick tamales, and these he powdered and stuffed into white socks and brown leather shoes.

The grandma's feet were lovely as pink pearls and dressed in velvety high heels that made her walk with a wobble, but she wore them anyway because they were pretty.

The baby's feet had ten tiny toes, pale and see-through like a salamander's, and these he popped into his mouth whenever he was hungry.

The mother's feet, plump and polite, descended like white pigeons from the sea of pillow, across the linoleum roses, down down the wooden stairs, over the chalk hopscotch squares, 5, 6, 7, blue sky.

Do you want this? And gave us a paper bag with one pair of lemon shoes and one red and one pair of dancing shoes that used to be white but were now pale blue. Here, and we said thank you and waited until she went upstairs.

Hurray! Today we are Cinderella because our feet fit exactly, and we laugh at Rachel's one foot with a girl's gray sock and a lady's high heel. Do you like these shoes? But the truth is it is scary to look down at your foot that is no longer yours and see attached a long long leg.

Everybody wants to trade. The lemon shoes for the red shoes, the red for the pair that were once white but are now pale blue, the pale blue for the lemon, and take them off and put them back on and keep on like this a long time until we are tired.

Then Lucy screams to take our socks off and yes, it's true. We have legs. Skinny and spotted with satin scars where scabs were picked, but legs, all our own, good to look at, and long.

It's Rachel who learns to walk the best all strutted in those magic high heels. She teaches us to cross and uncross our legs, and to run like a double-dutch rope, and how to walk down to the corner so that the shoes talk back to you with every step. Lucy, Rachel, me tee-tottering like so. Down to the corner where the men can't take their eyes off us. We must be Christmas.

Mr. Benny at the corner grocery puts down his important cigar: Your mother know you got shoes like that? Who give you those?

Nobody.

Them are dangerous, he says. You girls too young to be wearing shoes like that. Take them shoes off before I call the cops, but we just run.

On the avenue a boy on a homemade bicycle calls out: Ladies, lead me to heaven.

But there is nobody around but us.

Do you like these shoes? Rachel says yes, and Lucy says yes, and yes I say, these are the best shoes. We will never go back to wearing the other kind again. Do you like these shoes?

In front of the laundromat six girls with the same fat face pretend we are invisible. They are the cousins, Lucy says, and always jealous. We just keep strutting.

Across the street in front of the tavern a bum man on the stoop.

Do you like these shoes?

Bum man says, Yes, little girl. Your little lemon shoes are so beautiful. But come closer. I can't see very well. Come closer. Please.

You are a pretty girl, bum man continues. What's your name, pretty girl?

And Rachel says Rachel, just like that.

Now you know to talk to drunks is crazy and to tell them your name is worse, but who can blame her. She is young and dizzy to hear so many sweet things in one day, even if it is a bum man's whiskey words saying them.

Rachel, you are prettier than a yellow taxicab. You know that?

But we don't like it. We got to go, Lucy says.

If I give you a dollar will you kiss me? How about a dollar. I give you a dollar, and he looks in his pocket for wrinkled money.

We have to go right now, Lucy says taking Rachel's hand because she looks like she's thinking about that dollar.

Bum man is yelling something to the air but by now we are running fast and far away, our high heel shoes taking us all the way down the avenue and around the block, past the ugly cousins, past Mr. Benny's, up Mango Street, the back way, just in case.

We are tired of being beautiful. Lucy hides the lemon shoes and the red shoes and the shoes that used to be white but are now pale blue under a powerful bushel basket on the back porch, until one Tuesday her mother, who is very clean, throws them away. But no one complains.

A Rice Sandwich

The special kids, the ones who wear keys around their necks,
get to eat in the canteen. The canteen! Even the name sounds
important. And these kids at lunch time go there because
their mothers aren't home or home is too far away to get to.

My home isn't far but it's not close either, and somehow
I got it in my head one day to ask my mother to make me a
sandwich and write a note to the principal so I could eat in
the canteen too.

Oh no, she says pointing the butter knife at me as if I'm
starting trouble, no sir. Next thing you know everybody will
be wanting a bag lunch – I'll be up all night cutting bread
into little triangles, this one with mayonnaise, this one with
mustard, no pickles on mine, but mustard on one side please.
You kids just like to invent more work for me.

But Nenny says she doesn't want to eat at school – ever –
because she likes to go home with her best friend Gloria who
lives across the schoolyard. Gloria's mama has a big color
T.V. and all they do is watch cartoons. Kiki and Carlos, on
the other hand, are patrol boys. They don't want to eat at

school either. They like to stand out in the cold especially if it's raining. They think suffering is good for you ever since they saw that movie *300 Spartans*.

I'm no Spartan and hold up an anemic wrist to prove it. I can't even blow up a balloon without getting dizzy. And besides, I know how to make my own lunch. If I ate at school there'd be less dishes to wash. You would see me less and less and like me better. Every day at noon my chair would be empty. Where is my favorite daughter you would cry, and when I came home finally at three p.m. you would appreciate me.

Okay, Okay, my mother says after three days of this. And the following morning I get to go to school with my mother's letter and a rice sandwich because we don't have lunch meat.

Mondays or Fridays, it doesn't matter, mornings always go by slow and this day especially. But lunch time came finally and I got to get in line with the stay-at-school kids. Everything is fine until the nun who knows all the canteen kids by heart looks at me and says: You, who sent you here? And since I am shy, I don't say anything, just hold out my hand with the letter. This is no good, she says, till Sister Superior gives the okay. Go upstairs and see her. And so I went.

I had to wait for two kids in front of me to get hollered at, one because he did something in class, the other because he didn't. My turn came and I stood in front of the big desk with holy pictures under the glass while the Sister Superior read my letter. It went like this:

> Dear Sister Superior,
>   Please let Esperanza eat in the lunchroom because she lives too far away and she gets tired. As you can see she is very skinny. I hope to God she does not faint.
>
> > Thanking you,
> > Mrs. E. Cordero

You don't live far, she says. You live across the boulevard. That's only four blocks. Not even. Three maybe. Three long blocks away from here. I bet I can see your house from my window. Which one? Come here. Which one is your house?

And then she made me stand up on a box of books and point. That one? she said, pointing to a row of ugly three-flats, the ones even the raggedy men are ashamed to go into. Yes, I nodded even though I knew that wasn't my house and started to cry. I always cry when nuns yell at me, even if they're not yelling.

Then she was sorry and said I could stay – just for today, not tomorrow or the day after – you go home. And I said yes and could I please have a Kleenex – I had to blow my nose.

In the canteen, which was nothing special, lots of boys and girls watched while I cried and ate my sandwich, the bread already greasy and the rice cold.

Chanclas

It's me – Mama, Mama said. I open up and she's there with bags and big boxes, the new clothes and, yes, she's got the socks and a new slip with a little rose on it and a pink-and-white striped dress. What about the shoes? I forgot. Too late now. I'm tired. Whew!

Six-thirty already and my little cousin's baptism is over. All day waiting, the door locked, don't open up for nobody, and I don't till Mama gets back and buys everything except the shoes.

Now Uncle Nacho is coming in his car, and we have to hurry to get to Precious Blood Church quick because that's where the baptism party is, in the basement rented for today for dancing and tamales and everyone's kids running all over the place.

Mama dances, laughs, dances. All of a sudden, Mama is sick. I fan her hot face with a paper plate. Too many tamales, but Uncle Nacho says too many this and tilts his thumb to his lips.

Everybody laughing except me, because I'm wearing

the new dress, pink and white with stripes, and new under-clothes and new socks and the old saddle shoes I wear to school, brown and white, the kind I get every September be-cause they last long and they do. My feet scuffed and round, and the heels all crooked that look dumb with this dress, so I just sit.

Meanwhile that boy who is my cousin by first commun-ion or something asks me to dance and I can't. Just stuff my feet under the metal folding chair stamped Precious Blood and pick on a wad of brown gum that's stuck beneath the seat. I shake my head no. My feet growing bigger and bigger.

Then Uncle Nacho is pulling and pulling my arm and it doesn't matter how new the dress Mama bought is because my feet are ugly until my uncle who is a liar says, You are the prettiest girl here, will you dance, but I believe him, and yes, we are dancing, my Uncle Nacho and me, only I don't want to at first. My feet swell big and heavy like plungers, but I drag them across the linoleum floor straight center where Uncle wants to show off the new dance we learned. And Uncle spins me, and my skinny arms bend the way he taught me, and my mother watches, and my little cousins watch, and the boy who is my cousin by first communion watches, and everyone says, wow, who are those two who dance like in the movies, until I forget that I am wearing only ordinary shoes, brown and white, the kind my mother buys each year for school.

And all I hear is the clapping when the music stops. My uncle and me bow and he walks me back in my thick shoes to my mother who is proud to be my mother. All night the boy who is a man watches me dance. He watched me dance.

Hips

I like coffee, I like tea.
I like the boys and the boys like me.
Yes, no, maybe so. Yes, no, maybe so . . .

One day you wake up and they are there. Ready and waiting like a new Buick with the keys in the ignition. Ready to take you where?

They're good for holding a baby when you're cooking, Rachel says, turning the jump rope a little quicker. She has no imagination.

You need them to dance, says Lucy.

If you don't get them you may turn into a man. Nenny says this and she believes it. She is this way because of her age.

That's right, I add before Lucy or Rachel can make fun of her. She is stupid alright, but she *is* my sister.

But most important, hips are scientific, I say repeating what Alicia already told me. It's the bones that let you know which skeleton was a man's when it was a man and which a woman's.

They bloom like roses, I continue because it's obvious I'm the only one who can speak with any authority; I have science on my side. The bones just one day open. Just like that. One day you might decide to have kids, and then where are you going to put them? Got to have room. Bones got to give.

But don't have too many or your behind will spread. That's how it is, says Rachel whose mama is as wide as a boat. And we just laugh.

What I'm saying is who here is ready? You gotta be able to know what to do with hips when you get them, I say making it up as I go. You gotta know how to walk with hips, practice you know – like if half of you wanted to go one way and the other half the other.

That's to lullaby it, Nenny says, that's to rock the baby asleep inside you. And then she begins singing *seashells, copper bells, eevy, ivy, o-ver.*

I'm about to tell her that's the dumbest thing I've ever heard, but the more I think about it . . .

You gotta get the rhythm, and Lucy begins to dance. She has the idea, though she's having trouble keeping her end of the double-dutch steady.

It's gotta be just so, I say. Not too fast and not too slow. Not too fast and not too slow.

We slow the double circles down to a certain speed so Rachel who has just jumped in can practice shaking it.

I want to shake like hoochi-coochie, Lucy says. She is crazy.

I want to move like heebie-jeebie, I say picking up on the cue.

I want to be Tahiti. Or *merengue.* Or electricity.

Or *tembleque!*

Yes, *tembleque.* That's a good one.

And then it's Rachel who starts it:

Skip, skip,
snake in your hips.
Wiggle around
and break your lip.

Lucy waits a minute before her turn. She is thinking. Then she begins:

The waitress with the big fat hips
who pays the rent with taxi tips . . .
says nobody in town will kiss her on the lips
because . . .
because she looks like Christopher Columbus!
Yes, no, maybe so. Yes, no, maybe so.

She misses on maybe so. I take a little while before my turn, take a breath, and dive in:

Some are skinny like chicken lips.
Some are baggy like soggy Band-Aids
after you get out of the bathtub.
I don't care what kind I get.
Just as long as I get hips.

Everybody getting into it now except **Nenny** who is still humming *not a girl, not a boy, just a little baby.* She's like that.

When the two arcs open wide like jaws Nenny jumps in across from me, the rope tick-ticking, the little gold earrings our mama gave her for her First Holy Communion bouncing. She is the color of a bar of naphtha laundry soap, she is like the little brown piece left at the end of the wash, the hard little bone, my sister. Her mouth opens. She begins:

My mother and your mother were washing clothes.
My mother punched your mother right in the nose.
What color blood came out?

Not that old song, I say. You gotta use your own song. Make it up, you know? But she doesn't get it or won't. It's hard to say which. The rope turning, turning, turning.

Engine, engine number nine,
running down Chicago line.
If the train runs off the track
do you want your money back?
Do you want your MONEY back?
Yes, no, maybe so. Yes, no, maybe so . . .

I can tell Lucy and Rachel are disgusted, but they don't say anything because she's my sister.

Yes, no, maybe so. Yes, no, maybe so . . .

Nenny, I say, but she doesn't hear me. She is too many light-years away. She is in a world we don't belong to anymore. Nenny. Going. Going.

Y-E-S spells yes and out you go!

The First Job

It wasn't as if I didn't want to work. I did. I had even gone to the social security office the month before to get my social security number. I needed money. The Catholic high school cost a lot, and Papa said nobody went to public school unless you wanted to turn out bad.

I thought I'd find an easy job, the kind other kids had, working in the dime store or maybe a hotdog stand. And though I hadn't started looking yet, I thought I might the week after next. But when I came home that afternoon, all wet because Tito had pushed me into the open water hydrant – only I had sort of let him – Mama called me in the kitchen before I could even go and change, and Aunt Lala was sitting there drinking her coffee with a spoon. Aunt Lala said she had found a job for me at the Peter Pan Photo Finishers on North Broadway where she worked, and how old was I, and to show up tomorrow saying I was one year older, and that was that.

So the next morning I put on the navy blue dress that made me look older and borrowed money for lunch and bus fare because Aunt Lala said I wouldn't get paid till the next Friday, and I went in and saw the boss of the Peter Pan Photo Finishers on North Broadway where Aunt Lala worked and lied about my age like she told me to and sure enough, I started that same day.

In my job I had to wear white gloves. I was supposed to match negatives with their prints, just look at the picture and look for the same one on the negative strip, put it in the envelope, and do the next one. That's all. I didn't know where these envelopes were coming from or where they were going. I just did what I was told.

It was real easy, and I guess I wouldn't have minded it except that you got tired after a while and I didn't know if I could sit down or not, and then I started sitting down only when the two ladies next to me did. After a while they started to laugh and came up to me and said I could sit when I wanted to, and I said I knew.

When lunch time came, I was scared to eat alone in the company lunchroom with all those men and ladies looking, so I ate real fast standing in one of the washroom stalls and had lots of time left over, so I went back to work early. But then break time came, and not knowing where else to go, I went into the coatroom because there was a bench there.

I guess it was the time for the night shift or middle shift to arrive because a few people came in and punched the time clock, and an older Oriental man said hello and we talked for a while about my just starting, and he said we could be friends and next time to go in the lunchroom and sit with him, and I felt better. He had nice eyes and I didn't feel so nervous anymore. Then he asked if I knew what day it was, and when I said I didn't, he said it was his birthday and would I please give him a birthday kiss. I thought I would because he was so old and just as I was about to put my lips on his cheek, he grabs my face with both hands and kisses me hard on the mouth and doesn't let go.

Papa Who Wakes Up Tired in the Dark

Your *abuelito* is dead, Papa says early one morning in my room. *Está muerto*, and then as if he just heard the news himself, crumples like a coat and cries, my brave Papa cries. I have never seen my Papa cry and don't know what to do.

I know he will have to go away, that he will take a plane to Mexico, all the uncles and aunts will be there, and they will have a black-and-white photo taken in front of the tomb with flowers shaped like spears in a white vase because this is how they send the dead away in that country.

Because I am the oldest, my father has told me first, and now it is my turn to tell the others. I will have to explain why we can't play. I will have to tell them to be quiet today.

My Papa, his thick hands and thick shoes, who wakes up tired in the dark, who combs his hair with water, drinks his coffee, and is gone before we wake, today is sitting on my bed.

And I think if my own Papa died what would I do. I hold my Papa in my arms. I hold and hold and hold him.

Born Bad

Most likely I will go to hell and most likely I deserve to be there. My mother says I was born on an evil day and prays for me. Lucy and Rachel pray too. For ourselves and for each other . . . because of what we did to Aunt Lupe.

Her name was Guadalupe and she was pretty like my mother. Dark. Good to look at. In her Joan Crawford dress and swimmer's legs. Aunt Lupe of the photographs.

But I knew her sick from the disease that would not go, her legs bunched under the yellow sheets, the bones gone limp as worms. The yellow pillow, the yellow smell, the bottles and spoons. Her head thrown back like a thirsty lady. My aunt, the swimmer.

Hard to imagine her legs once strong, the bones hard and parting water, clean sharp strokes, not bent and wrinkled like a baby, not drowning under the sticky yellow light. Second-floor rear apartment. The naked light bulb. The high ceilings. The light bulb always burning.

I don't know who decides who deserves to go bad. There was no evil in her birth. No wicked curse. One day

I believe she was swimming, and the next day she was sick. It might have been the day that gray photograph was taken. It might have been the day she was holding cousin Totchy and baby Frank. It might have been the moment she pointed to the camera for the kids to look and they wouldn't.

Maybe the sky didn't look the day she fell down. Maybe God was busy. It could be true she didn't dive right one day and hurt her spine. Or maybe the story that she fell very hard from a high step stool, like Totchy said, is true.

But I think diseases have no eyes. They pick with a dizzy finger anyone, just anyone. Like my aunt who happened to be walking down the street one day in her Joan Crawford dress, in her funny felt hat with the black feather, cousin Totchy in one hand, baby Frank in the other.

Sometimes you get used to the sick and sometimes the sickness, if it is there too long, gets to seem normal. This is how it was with her, and maybe this is why we chose her.

It was a game, that's all. It was the game we played every afternoon ever since that day one of us invented it – I can't remember who – I think it was me.

You had to pick somebody. You had to think of someone everybody knew. Someone you could imitate and everyone else would have to guess who it was. It started out with famous people: Wonder Woman, the Beatles, Marilyn Monroe. . . . But then somebody thought it'd be better if we changed the game a little, if we pretended we were Mr. Benny, or his wife Blanca, or Ruthie, or anybody we knew.

I don't know why we picked her. Maybe we were bored that day. Maybe we got tired. We liked my aunt. She listened to our stories. She always asked us to come back. Lucy, me, Rachel. I hated to go there alone. The six blocks to the dark apartment, second-floor rear building where sunlight never came, and what did it matter? My aunt was blind by then. She never saw the dirty dishes in the sink. She couldn't see the ceilings dusty with flies, the ugly maroon walls, the bottles and sticky spoons. I can't forget the smell. Like sticky capsules filled with jelly. My aunt, a little oyster, a little piece of meat on an open shell for us to look at. Hello, hello. As if she had fallen into a well.

I took my library books to her house. I read her stories. I liked the book *The Waterbabies*. She liked it too. I never knew how sick she was until that day I tried to show her one of the pictures in the book, a beautiful color picture of the water babies swimming in the sea. I held the book up to her face. I can't see it, she said, I'm blind. And then I was ashamed.

She listened to every book, every poem I read her. One day I read her one of my own. I came very close. I whispered it into the pillow:

> I want to be
> like the waves on the sea,
> like the clouds in the wind,
> but I'm me.
> One day I'll jump
> out of my skin.
> I'll shake the sky
> like a hundred violins.

That's nice. That's very good, she said in her tired voice. You just remember to keep writing, Esperanza. You must keep writing. It will keep you free, and I said yes, but at that time I didn't know what she meant.

The day we played the game, we didn't know she was going to die. We pretended with our heads thrown back, our arms limp and useless, dangling like the dead. We laughed the way she did. We talked the way she talked, the way blind people talk without moving their head. We imitated the way you had to lift her head a little so she could drink water, she sucked it up slow out of a green tin cup. The water was warm and tasted like metal. Lucy laughed. Rachel too. We took turns being her. We screamed in the weak voice of a parrot for Totchy to come and wash those dishes. It was easy.

We didn't know. She had been dying such a long time, we forgot. Maybe she was ashamed. Maybe she was embarrassed it took so many years. The kids who wanted to be kids instead of washing dishes and ironing their papa's shirts, and the husband who wanted a wife again.

And then she died, my aunt who listened to my poems.

And then we began to dream the dreams.

Elenita, Cards, Palm, Water

Elenita, witch woman, wipes the table with a rag because Ernie who is feeding the baby spilled Kool-Aid. She says: Take that crazy baby out of here and drink your Kool-Aid in the living room. Can't you see I'm busy? Ernie takes the baby into the living room where Bugs Bunny is on T.V.

Good lucky you didn't come yesterday, she says. The planets were all mixed up yesterday.

Her T.V. is color and big and all her pretty furniture made out of red fur like the teddy bears they give away in carnivals. She has them covered with plastic. I think this is on account of the baby.

Yes, it's a good thing, I say.

But we stay in the kitchen because this is where she works. The top of the refrigerator busy with holy candles, some lit, some not, red and green and blue, a plaster saint and a dusty Palm Sunday cross, and a picture of the voodoo hand taped to the wall.

Get the water, she says.

I go to the sink and pick the only clean glass there, a beer mug that says the beer that made Milwaukee famous, and fill it up with hot water from the tap, then put the glass of water on the center of the table, the way she taught me.

Look in it, do you see anything?

But all I see are bubbles.

You see anybody's face?

Nope, just bubbles, I say.

That's okay, and she makes the sign of the cross over the water three times and then begins to cut the cards.

They're not like ordinary playing cards, these cards. They're strange, with blond men on horses and crazy baseball bats with thorns. Golden goblets, sad-looking women dressed in old-fashioned dresses, and roses that cry.

There is a good Bugs Bunny cartoon on T.V. I know, I saw it before and recognize the music and wish I could go sit on the plastic couch with Ernie and the baby, but now my fortune begins. My whole life on that kitchen table: past, present, future. Then she takes my hand and looks into my palm. Closes it. Closes her eyes too.

Do you feel it, feel the cold?

Yes, I lie, but only a little.

Good, she says, *los espíritus* are here. And begins.

This card, the one with the dark man on a dark horse, this means jealousy, and this one, sorrow. Here a pillar of bees and this a mattress of luxury. You will go to a wedding soon and did you lose an anchor of arms, yes, an anchor of arms? It's clear that's what that means.

What about a house, I say, because that's what I came for.

Ah, yes, a home in the heart. I see a home in the heart.

Is that *it?*

That's what I see, she says, then gets up because the kids are fighting. Elenita gets up to hit and then hug them. She really does love them, only sometimes they are rude.

She comes back and can tell I'm disappointed. She's a witch woman and knows many things. If you got a headache, rub a cold egg across your face. Need to forget an old romance? Take a chicken's foot, tie it with red string, spin it over your head three times, then burn it. Bad spirits keeping you awake? Sleep next to a holy candle for seven days, then on the eighth day, spit. And lots of other stuff. Only now she can tell I'm sad.

Baby, I'll look again if you want me to. And she looks again into the cards, palm, water, and says uh-huh.

A home in the heart, I was right.

Only I don't get it.

A new house, a house made of heart. I'll light a candle for you.

All this for five dollars I give her.

Thank you and goodbye and be careful of the evil eye. Come back again on a Thursday when the stars are stronger. And may the Virgin bless you. And shuts the door.

Geraldo No Last Name

She met him at a dance. Pretty too, and young. Said he worked in a restaurant, but she can't remember which one. Geraldo. That's all. Green pants and Saturday shirt. Geraldo. That's what he told her.

And how was she to know she'd be the last one to see him alive. An accident, don't you know. Hit-and-run. Marin, she goes to all those dances. Uptown. Logan. Embassy. Palmer. Aragon. Fontana. The Manor. She likes to dance. She knows how to do cumbias and salsas and rancheras even. And he was just someone she danced with. Somebody she met that night. That's right.

That's the story. That's what she said again and again. Once to the hospital people and twice to the police. No address. No name. Nothing in his pockets. Ain't it a shame.

Only Marin can't explain why it mattered, the hours and hours, for somebody she didn't even know. The hospital emergency room. Nobody but an intern working all alone. And maybe if the surgeon would've come, maybe if he hadn't lost so much blood, if the surgeon had only come, they would know who to notify and where.

But what difference does it make? He wasn't anything to her. He wasn't her boyfriend or anything like that. Just another *brazer* who didn't speak English. Just another wetback. You know the kind. The ones who always look ashamed. And what was she doing out at three a.m. anyway? Marin who was sent home with her coat and some aspirin. How does she explain?

She met him at a dance. Geraldo in his shiny shirt and green pants. Geraldo going to a dance.

What does it matter?

They never saw the kitchenettes. They never knew about the two-room flats and sleeping rooms he rented, the weekly money orders sent home, the currency exchange. How could they?

His name was Geraldo. And his home is in another country. The ones he left behind are far away, will wonder, shrug, remember. Geraldo – he went north . . . we never heard from him again.

Edna's Ruthie

Ruthie, tall skinny lady with red lipstick and blue ba-
bushka, one blue sock and one green because she forgot, is
the only grown-up we know who likes to play. She takes
her dog Bobo for a walk and laughs all by herself, that
Ruthie. She doesn't need anybody to laugh with, she just
laughs.

She is Edna's daughter, the lady who owns the big building next door, three apartments front and back. Every week
Edna is screaming at somebody, and every week somebody
has to move away. Once she threw out a pregnant lady just
because she owned a duck . . . and it was a nice duck too.
But Ruthie lives here and Edna can't throw her out because
Ruthie is her daughter.

Ruthie came one day, it seemed, out of nowhere. Angel
Vargas was trying to teach us how to whistle. Then we heard
someone whistling – beautiful like the Emperor's nightin-
gale – and when we turned around there was Ruthie.

Sometimes we go shopping and take her with us, but
she never comes inside the stores and if she does she keeps

looking around her like a wild animal in a house for the first time.

She likes candy. When we go to Mr. Benny's grocery she gives us money to buy her some. She says make sure it's the soft kind because her teeth hurt. Then she promises to see the dentist next week, but when next week comes, she doesn't go.

Ruthie sees lovely things everywhere. I might be telling her a joke and she'll stop and say: The moon is beautiful like a balloon. Or somebody might be singing and she'll point to a few clouds: Look, Marlon Brando. Or a sphinx winking. Or my left shoe.

Once some friends of Edna's came to visit and asked Ruthie if she wanted to go with them to play bingo. The car motor was running, and Ruthie stood on the steps wondering whether to go. Should I go, Ma? she asked the gray shadow behind the second-floor screen. I don't care, says the screen, go if you want. Ruthie looked at the ground. What do you think, Ma? Do what you want, how should I know? Ruthie looked at the ground some more. The car with the motor running waited fifteen minutes and then they left. When we brought out the deck of cards that night, we let Ruthie deal.

There were many things Ruthie could have been if she wanted to. Not only is she a good whistler, but she can sing and dance too. She had lots of job offers when she was young, but she never took them. She got married instead and moved away to a pretty house outside the city. Only thing I can't understand is why Ruthie is living on Mango Street if she doesn't have to, why is she sleeping on a couch in her mother's living room when she has a real house all her own, but she says she's just visiting and next weekend her husband's going to take her home. But the weekends come and go and Ruthie stays. No matter. We are glad because she is our friend.

I like showing Ruthie the books I take out of the library. Books are wonderful, Ruthie says, and then she runs her hand over them as if she could read them in braille. They're wonderful, wonderful, but I can't read anymore. I get headaches. I need to go to the eye doctor next week. I used to write children's books once, did I tell you?

One day I memorized all of "The Walrus and the Carpenter" because I wanted Ruthie to hear me. "The sun was shining on the sea, shining with all his might . . ." Ruthie looked at the sky and her eyes got watery at times. Finally I came to the last lines: "But answer came there none – and this was scarcely odd, because they'd eaten every one . . ." She took a long time looking at me before she opened her mouth, and then she said, You have the most beautiful teeth I have ever seen, and went inside.

The Earl of Tennessee

Earl lives next door in Edna's basement, behind the flower boxes Edna paints green each year, behind the dusty geraniums. We used to sit on the flower boxes until the day Tito saw a cockroach with a spot of green paint on its head. Now we sit on the steps that swing around the basement apartment where Earl lives.

Earl works nights. His blinds are always closed during the day. Sometimes he comes out and tells us to keep quiet. The little wooden door that has wedged shut the dark for so long opens with a sigh and lets out a breath of mold and dampness, like books that have been left out in the rain. This is the only time we see Earl except for when he comes and goes to work. He has two little black dogs that go everywhere with him. They don't walk like ordinary dogs, but leap and somersault like an apostrophe and comma.

At night Nenny and I can hear when Earl comes home from work. First the click and whine of the car door opening, then the scrape of concrete, the excited tinkling of dog tags, followed by the heavy jingling of keys, and finally the moan of the wooden door as it opens and lets loose its sigh of dampness.

Earl is a jukebox repairman. He learned his trade in the South, he says. He speaks with a Southern accent, smokes fat cigars and wears a felt hat – winter or summer, hot or cold, don't matter – a felt hat. In his apartment are boxes and boxes of 45 records, moldy and damp like the smell that comes out of his apartment whenever he opens the door. He gives the records away to us – all except the country and western.

The word is that Earl is married and has a wife some-where. Edna says she saw her once when Earl brought her to the apartment. Mama says she is a skinny thing, blond and pale like salamanders that have never seen the sun. But I saw her once too and she's not that way at all. And the boys across the street say she is a tall red-headed lady who wears tight pink pants and green glasses. We never agree on what she looks like, but we do know this. Whenever she arrives, he holds her tight by the crook of the arm. They walk fast into the apartment, lock the door behind them and never stay long.

Sire

I don't remember when I first noticed him looking at me – Sire. But I knew he was looking. Every time. All the time I walked past his house. Him and his friends sitting on their bikes in front of the house, pitching pennies. They didn't scare me. They did, but I wouldn't let them know. I don't cross the street like other girls. Straight ahead, straight eyes. I walked past. I knew he was looking. I had to prove to me I wasn't scared of nobody's eyes, not even his. I had to look back hard, just once, like he was glass. And I did. I did once. But I looked too long when he rode his bike past me. I looked because I wanted to be brave, straight into the dusty cat fur of his eyes and the bike stopped and he bumped into a parked car, bumped, and I walked fast. It made your blood freeze to have somebody look at you like that. Somebody looked at me. Somebody looked. But his kind, his ways. He is a punk, Papa says, and Mama says not to talk to him.

And then his girlfriend came. Lois I heard him call her. She is tiny and pretty and smells like baby's skin. I see her sometimes running to the store for him. And once when she was standing next to me at Mr. Benny's grocery she was barefoot, and I saw her barefoot baby toenails all painted pale pale pink, like little pink seashells, and she smells pink like babies do. She's got big girl hands, and her bones are long like ladies' bones, and she wears makeup too. But she doesn't know how to tie her shoes. I do.

Sometimes I hear them laughing late, beer cans and cats and the trees talking to themselves: wait, wait, wait. Sire lets Lois ride his bike around the block, or they take walks together. I watch them. She holds his hand, and he stops sometimes to tie her shoes. But Mama says those kinds of girls, those girls are the ones that go into alleys. Lois who can't tie her shoes. Where does he take her?

Everything is holding its breath inside me. Everything is waiting to explode like Christmas. I want to be all new and shiny. I want to sit out bad at night, a boy around my neck and the wind under my skirt. Not this way, every evening talking to the trees, leaning out my window, imagining what I can't see.

A boy held me once so hard, I swear, I felt the grip and weight of his arms, but it was a dream.

Sire. How did you hold her? Was it? Like this? And when you kissed her? Like this?

Four Skinny Trees

They are the only ones who understand me. I am the only one who understands them. Four skinny trees with skinny necks and pointy elbows like mine. Four who do not belong here but are here. Four raggedy excuses planted by the city. From our room we can hear them, but Nenny just sleeps and doesn't appreciate these things.

Their strength is secret. They send ferocious roots beneath the ground. They grow up and they grow down and grab the earth between their hairy toes and bite the sky with violent teeth and never quit their anger. This is how they keep.

Let one forget his reason for being, they'd all droop like tulips in a glass, each with their arms around the other. Keep, keep, keep, trees say when I sleep. They teach.

When I am too sad and too skinny to keep keeping, when I am a tiny thing against so many bricks, then it is I look at trees. When there is nothing left to look at on this street. Four who grew despite concrete. Four who reach and do not forget to reach. Four whose only reason is to be and be.

No Speak English

Mamacita is the big mama of the man across the street, third-floor front. Rachel says her name ought to be *Mamasota*, but I think that's mean.

The man saved his money to bring her here. He saved and saved because she was alone with the baby boy in that country. He worked two jobs. He came home late and he left early. Every day.

Then one day *Mamacita* and the baby boy arrived in a yellow taxi. The taxi door opened like a waiter's arm. Out stepped a tiny pink shoe, a foot soft as a rabbit's ear, then the thick ankle, a flutter of hips, fuchsia roses and green perfume. The man had to pull her, the taxicab driver had to push. Push, pull. Push, pull. Poof!

All at once she bloomed. Huge, enormous, beautiful to look at, from the salmon-pink feather on the tip of her hat down to the little rosebuds of her toes. I couldn't take my eyes off her tiny shoes.

Up, up, up the stairs she went with the baby boy in a blue blanket, the man carrying her suitcases, her lavender hatboxes, a dozen boxes of satin high heels. Then we didn't see her.

Somebody said because she's too fat, somebody because of the three flights of stairs, but I believe she doesn't come out because she is afraid to speak English, and maybe this is so since she only knows eight words. She knows to say: *He not here* for when the landlord comes, *No speak English* if anybody else comes, and *Holy smokes*. I don't know where she learned this, but I heard her say it one time and it surprised me.

My father says when he came to this country he ate hamandeggs for three months. Breakfast, lunch and dinner. Hamandeggs. That was the only word he knew. He doesn't eat hamandeggs anymore.

Whatever her reasons, whether she is fat, or can't climb the stairs, or is afraid of English, she won't come down. She sits all day by the window and plays the Spanish radio show and sings all the homesick songs about her country in a voice that sounds like a seagull.

Home. Home. Home is a house in a photograph, a pink house, pink as hollyhocks with lots of startled light. The man paints the walls of the apartment pink, but it's not the same, you know. She still sighs for her pink house, and then I think she cries. I would.

Sometimes the man gets disgusted. He starts screaming and you can hear it all the way down the street.

Ay, she says, she is sad.

Oh, he says. Not again.

¿Cuándo, cuándo, cuándo? she asks.

¡Ay, caray! We *are* home. This *is* home. Here I am and here I stay. Speak English. Speak English. Christ!

¡Ay! Mamacita, who does not belong, every once in a while lets out a cry, hysterical, high, as if he had torn the only skinny thread that kept her alive, the only road out to that country.

And then to break her heart forever, the baby boy, who

has begun to talk, starts to sing the Pepsi commercial he heard on T.V.

No speak English, she says to the child who is singing in the language that sounds like tin. No speak English, no speak English, and bubbles into tears. No, no, no, as if she can't believe her ears.

Rafaela Who Drinks Coconut &
Papaya Juice on Tuesdays

On Tuesdays Rafaela's husband comes home late because
that's the night he plays dominoes. And then Rafaela, who
is still young but getting old from leaning out the window
so much, gets locked indoors because her husband is afraid
Rafaela will run away since she is too beautiful to look at.

Rafaela leans out the window and leans on her elbow and
dreams her hair is like Rapunzel's. On the corner there is
music from the bar, and Rafaela wishes she could go there
and dance before she gets old.

A long time passes and we forget she is up there watching
until she says: Kids, if I give you a dollar will you go to the
store and buy me something? She throws a crumpled dollar
down and always asks for coconut or sometimes papaya juice,
and we send it up to her in a paper shopping bag she lets
down with clothesline.

Rafaela who drinks and drinks coconut and papaya juice
on Tuesdays and wishes there were sweeter drinks, not bitter
like an empty room, but sweet sweet like the island, like the
dance hall down the street where women much older than

her throw green eyes easily like dice and open homes with keys. And always there is someone offering sweeter drinks, someone promising to keep them on a silver string.

Sally

Sally is the girl with eyes like Egypt and nylons the color of smoke. The boys at school think she's beautiful because her hair is shiny black like raven feathers and when she laughs, she flicks her hair back like a satin shawl over her shoulders and laughs.

Her father says to be this beautiful is trouble. They are very strict in his religion. They are not supposed to dance. He remembers his sisters and is sad. Then she can't go out. Sally I mean.

Sally, who taught you to paint your eyes like Cleopatra? And if I roll the little brush with my tongue and chew it to a point and dip it in the muddy cake, the one in the little red box, will you teach me?

I like your black coat and those shoes you wear, where did you get them? My mother says to wear black so young is dangerous, but I want to buy shoes just like yours, like your black ones made out of suede, just like those. And one day, when my mother's in a good mood, maybe after my next birthday, I'm going to ask to buy the nylons too.

Cheryl, who is not your friend anymore, not since last Tuesday before Easter, not since the day you made her ear bleed, not since she called you that name and bit a hole in your arm and you looked as if you were going to cry and everyone was waiting and you didn't, you didn't, Sally, not since then, you don't have a best friend to lean against the schoolyard fence with, to laugh behind your hands at what the boys say. There is no one to lend you her hairbrush.

The stories the boys tell in the coatroom, they're not true. You lean against the schoolyard fence alone with your eyes closed as if no one was watching, as if no one could see you standing there, Sally. What do you think about when you close your eyes like that? And why do you always have to go straight home after school? You become a different Sally. You pull your skirt straight, you rub the blue paint off your eyelids. You don't laugh, Sally. You look at your feet and walk fast to the house you can't come out from.

Sally, do you sometimes wish you didn't have to go home? Do you wish your feet would one day keep walking and take you far away from Mango Street, far away and maybe your feet would stop in front of a house, a nice one with flowers and big windows and steps for you to climb up two by two upstairs to where a room is waiting for you. And if you opened the little window latch and gave it a shove, the windows would swing open, all the sky would come in. There'd be no nosy neighbors watching, no motorcycles and cars, no sheets and towels and laundry. Only trees and more trees and plenty of blue sky. And you could laugh, Sally. You could go to sleep and wake up and never have to think who likes and doesn't like you. You could close your eyes and you wouldn't have to worry what people said because you never belonged here anyway and nobody could make you sad and nobody would think you're strange be-cause you like to dream and dream. And no one could yell at you if they saw you out in the dark leaning against a car, leaning against somebody without someone thinking you are bad, without somebody saying it is wrong, without the whole world waiting for you to make a mistake when all you wanted, all you wanted, Sally, was to love and to love and to love and to love, and no one could call that crazy.

Minerva Writes Poems

Minerva is only a little bit older than me but already she has two kids and a husband who left. Her mother raised her kids alone and it looks like her daughters will go that way too. Minerva cries because her luck is unlucky. Every night and every day. And prays. But when the kids are asleep after she's fed them their pancake dinner, she writes poems on little pieces of paper that she folds over and over and holds in her hands a long time, little pieces of paper that smell like a dime.

She lets me read her poems. I let her read mine. She is always sad like a house on fire – always something wrong. She has many troubles, but the big one is her husband who left and keeps leaving.

One day she is through and lets him know enough is enough. Out the door he goes. Clothes, records, shoes. Out the window and the door locked. But that night he comes back and sends a big rock through the window. Then he is sorry and she opens the door again. Same story.

Next week she comes over black and blue and asks what can she do? Minerva. I don't know which way she'll go. There is nothing *I* can do.

Bums in the Attic

I want a house on a hill like the ones with the gardens where Papa works. We go on Sundays, Papa's day off. I used to go. I don't anymore. You don't like to go out with us, Papa says. Getting too old? Getting too stuck-up, says Nenny. I don't tell them I am ashamed – all of us staring out the window like the hungry. I am tired of looking at what we can't have. When we win the lottery . . . Mama begins, and then I stop listening.

People who live on hills sleep so close to the stars they forget those of us who live too much on earth. They don't look down at all except to be content to live on hills. They have nothing to do with last week's garbage or fear of rats. Night comes. Nothing wakes them but the wind.

One day I'll own my own house, but I won't forget who I am or where I came from. Passing bums will ask, Can I come in? I'll offer them the attic, ask them to stay, because I know how it is to be without a house.

Some days after dinner, guests and I will sit in front of a fire. Floorboards will squeak upstairs. The attic grumble.

Rats? they'll ask.

Bums, I'll say, and I'll be happy.

Beautiful & Cruel

I am an ugly daughter. I am the one nobody comes for.

Nenny says she won't wait her whole life for a husband to come and get her, that Minerva's sister left her mother's house by having a baby, but she doesn't want to go that way either. She wants things all her own, to pick and choose. Nenny has pretty eyes and it's easy to talk that way if you are pretty.

My mother says when I get older my dusty hair will settle and my blouse will learn to stay clean, but I have decided not to grow up tame like the others who lay their necks on the threshold waiting for the ball and chain.

In the movies there is always one with red red lips who is beautiful and cruel. She is the one who drives the men crazy and laughs them all away. Her power is her own. She will not give it away.

I have begun my own quiet war. Simple. Sure. I am one who leaves the table like a man, without putting back the chair or picking up the plate.

A Smart Cookie

I could've been somebody, you know? my mother says and sighs. She has lived in this city her whole life. She can speak two languages. She can sing an opera. She knows how to fix a T.V. But she doesn't know which subway train to take to get downtown. I hold her hand very tight while we wait for the right train to arrive.

She used to draw when she had time. Now she draws with a needle and thread, little knotted rosebuds, tulips made of silk thread. Someday she would like to go to the ballet. Someday she would like to see a play. She borrows opera records from the public library and sings with velvety lungs powerful as morning glories.

Today while cooking oatmeal she is Madame Butterfly until she sighs and points the wooden spoon at me. I could've been somebody, you know? Esperanza, you go to school. Study hard. That Madame Butterfly was a fool. She stirs the oatmeal. Look at my *comadres*. She means Izaura whose husband left and Yolanda whose husband is dead. Got to take care all your own, she says shaking her head.

Then out of nowhere:

Shame is a bad thing, you know. It keeps you down. You want to know why I quit school? Because I didn't have nice clothes. No clothes, but I had brains.

Yup, she says disgusted, stirring again. I was a smart cookie then.

What Sally Said

He never hits me hard. She said her mama rubs lard on all the places where it hurts. Then at school she'd say she fell. That's where all the blue places come from. That's why her skin is always scarred.

But who believes her. A girl that big, a girl who comes in with her pretty face all beaten and black can't be falling off the stairs. He never hits me hard.

But Sally doesn't tell about that time he hit her with his hands just like a dog, she said, like if I was an animal. He thinks I'm going to run away like his sisters who made the family ashamed. Just because I'm a daughter, and then she doesn't say.

Sally was going to get permission to stay with us a little and one Thursday she came finally with a sack full of clothes and a paper bag of sweetbread her mama sent. And would've stayed too except when the dark came her father, whose eyes were little from crying, knocked on the door and said please come back, this is the last time. And she said Daddy and went home.

Then we didn't need to worry. Until one day Sally's father catches her talking to a boy and the next day she doesn't come to school. And the next. Until the way Sally tells it, he just went crazy, he just forgot he was her father between the buckle and the belt.

You're not my daughter, you're not my daughter. And then he broke into his hands.

The Monkey Garden

The monkey doesn't live there anymore. The monkey moved – to Kentucky – and took his people with him. And I was glad because I couldn't listen anymore to his wild screaming at night, the twangy yakkety-yak of the people who owned him. The green metal cage, the porcelain table top, the family that spoke like guitars. Monkey, family, table. All gone.

And it was then we took over the garden we had been afraid to go into when the monkey screamed and showed its yellow teeth.

There were sunflowers big as flowers on Mars and thick cockscombs bleeding the deep red fringe of theater curtains. There were dizzy bees and bow-tied fruit flies turning somersaults and humming in the air. Sweet sweet peach trees. Thorn roses and thistle and pears. Weeds like so many squinty-eyed stars and brush that made your ankles itch and itch until you washed with soap and water. There were big green apples hard as knees. And everywhere the sleepy smell of rotting wood, damp earth and dusty hollyhocks thick and perfumy like the blue-blond hair of the dead.

Yellow spiders ran when we turned rocks over and pale worms blind and afraid of light rolled over in their sleep. Poke a stick in the sandy soil and a few blue-skinned beetles would appear, an avenue of ants, so many crusty lady bugs. This was a garden, a wonderful thing to look at in the spring. But bit by bit, after the monkey left, the garden began to take over itself. Flowers stopped obeying the little bricks that kept them from growing beyond their paths. Weeds mixed in. Dead cars appeared overnight like mushrooms. First one and then another and then a pale blue pickup with the front windshield missing. Before you knew it, the monkey garden became filled with sleepy cars.

Things had a way of disappearing in the garden, as if the garden itself ate them, or, as if with its old-man memory, it put them away and forgot them. Nenny found a dollar and a dead mouse between two rocks in the stone wall where the morning glories climbed, and once when we were playing hide-and-seek, Eddie Vargas laid his head beneath a hibiscus tree and fell asleep there like a Rip Van Winkle until somebody remembered he was in the game and went back to look for him.

This, I suppose, was the reason why we went there. Far away from where our mothers could find us. We and a few old dogs who lived inside the empty cars. We made a clubhouse once on the back of that old blue pickup. And besides, we liked to jump from the roof of one car to another and pretend they were giant mushrooms.

Somebody started the lie that the monkey garden had been there before anything. We liked to think the garden could hide things for a thousand years. There beneath the roots of soggy flowers were the bones of murdered pirates and dinosaurs, the eye of a unicorn turned to coal.

This is where I wanted to die and where I tried one day but not even the monkey garden would have me. It was the last day I would go there.

Who was it that said I was getting too old to play the games? Who was it I didn't listen to? I only remember that when the others ran, I wanted to run too, up and down and through the monkey garden, fast as the boys, not like Sally who screamed if she got her stockings muddy.

I said, Sally, come on, but she wouldn't. She stayed by the curb talking to Tito and his friends. Play with the kids if you want, she said, I'm staying here. She could be stuck-up like that if she wanted to, so I just left.

It was her own fault too. When I got back Sally was pretending to be mad . . . something about the boys having stolen her keys. Please give them back to me, she said punching the nearest one with a soft fist. They were laughing. She was too. It was a joke I didn't get.

I wanted to go back with the other kids who were still jumping on cars, still chasing each other through the garden, but Sally had her own game.

One of the boys invented the rules. One of Tito's friends said you can't get the keys back unless you kiss us and Sally pretended to be mad at first but she said yes. It was that simple.

I don't know why, but something inside me wanted to throw a stick. Something wanted to say no when I watched Sally going into the garden with Tito's buddies all grinning. It was just a kiss, that's all. A kiss for each one. So what, she said.

Only how come I felt angry inside. Like something wasn't right. Sally went behind that old blue pickup to kiss the boys and get her keys back, and I ran up three flights of stairs to where Tito lived. His mother was ironing shirts. She was sprinkling water on them from an empty pop bottle and smoking a cigarette.

Your son and his friends stole Sally's keys and now they won't give them back unless she kisses them and right now they're making her kiss them, I said all out of breath from the three flights of stairs.

Those kids, she said, not looking up from her ironing.

That's all?

What do you want me to do, she said, call the cops? And kept on ironing.

I looked at her a long time, but couldn't think of anything to say, and ran back down the three flights to the garden where Sally needed to be saved. I took three big sticks and a brick and figured this was enough.

But when I got there Sally said go home. Those boys said leave us alone. I felt stupid with my brick. They all looked at me as if *I* was the one that was crazy and made me feel ashamed.

And then I don't know why but I had to run away. I had to hide myself at the other end of the garden, in the jungle part, under a tree that wouldn't mind if I lay down and cried a long time. I closed my eyes like tight stars so that I wouldn't, but I did. My face felt hot. Everything inside hiccupped.

I read somewhere in India there are priests who can will their heart to stop beating. I wanted to will my blood to stop, my heart to quit its pumping. I wanted to be dead, to turn into the rain, my eyes melt into the ground like two black snails. I wished and wished. I closed my eyes and willed it, but when I got up my dress was green and I had a headache.

I looked at my feet in their white socks and ugly round shoes. They seemed far away. They didn't seem to be my feet anymore. And the garden that had been such a good place to play didn't seem mine either.

Red Clowns

Sally, you lied. It wasn't what you said at all. What he did. Where he touched me. I didn't want it, Sally. The way they said it, the way it's supposed to be, all the storybooks and movies, why did you lie to me?

I was waiting by the red clowns. I was standing by the tilt-a-whirl where you said. And anyway I don't like carnivals. I went to be with you because you laugh on the tilt-a-whirl, you throw your head back and laugh. I hold your change, wave, count how many times you go by. Those boys that look at you because you're pretty. I like to be with you, Sally. You're my friend. But that big boy, where did he take you? I waited such a long time. I waited by the red clowns, just like you said, but you never came, you never came for me.

Sally Sally a hundred times. Why didn't you hear me when I called? Why didn't you tell them to leave me alone? The one who grabbed me by the arm, he wouldn't let me go. He said I love you, Spanish girl, I love you, and pressed his sour mouth to mine.

Sally, make him stop. I couldn't make them go away.

I couldn't do anything but cry. I don't remember. It was dark. I don't remember. I don't remember. Please don't make me tell it all.

Why did you leave me all alone? I waited my whole life. You're a liar. They all lied. All the books and magazines, everything that told it wrong. Only his dirty fingernails against my skin, only his sour smell again. The moon that watched. The tilt-a-whirl. The red clowns laughing their thick-tongue laugh.

Then the colors began to whirl. Sky tipped. Their high black gym shoes ran. Sally, you lied, you lied. He wouldn't let me go. He said I love you, I love you, Spanish girl.

Linoleum Roses

Sally got married like we knew she would, young and not ready but married just the same. She met a marshmallow salesman at a school bazaar, and she married him in another state where it's legal to get married before eighth grade. She has her husband and her house now, her pillowcases and her plates. She says she is in love, but I think she did it to escape.

Sally says she likes being married because now she gets to buy her own things when her husband gives her money. She is happy, except sometimes her husband gets angry and once he broke the door where his foot went through, though most days he is okay. Except he won't let her talk on the telephone. And he doesn't let her look out the window. And he doesn't like her friends, so nobody gets to visit her unless he is working.

She sits at home because she is afraid to go outside without his permission. She looks at all the things they own: the towels and the toaster, the alarm clock and the drapes. She likes looking at the walls, at how neatly their corners meet, the linoleum roses on the floor, the ceiling smooth as wedding cake.

The Three Sisters

They came with the wind that blows in August, thin as a spider web and barely noticed. Three who did not seem to be related to anything but the moon. One with laughter like tin and one with eyes of a cat and one with hands like porcelain. The aunts, the three sisters, *las comadres*, they said.

The baby died. Lucy and Rachel's sister. One night a dog cried, and the next day a yellow bird flew in through an open window. Before the week was over, the baby's fever was worse. Then Jesus came and took the baby with him far away. That's what their mother said.

Then the visitors came . . . in and out of the little house. It was hard to keep the floors clean. Anybody who had ever wondered what color the walls were came and came to look at that little thumb of a human in a box like candy.

I had never seen the dead before, not for real, not in somebody's living room for people to kiss and bless themselves and light a candle for. Not in a house. It seemed strange.

They must've known, the sisters. They had the power and could sense what was what. They said, Come here, and gave me a stick of gum. They smelled like Kleenex or the inside of a satin handbag, and then I didn't feel afraid.

What's your name, the cat-eyed one asked.

Esperanza, I said.

Esperanza, the old blue-veined one repeated in a high thin voice. Esperanza . . . a good good name.

My knees hurt, the one with the funny laugh complained. Tomorrow it will rain.

Yes, tomorrow, they said.

How do you know? I asked.

We know.

Look at her hands, cat-eyed said.

And they turned them over and over as if they were looking for something.

She's special.

Yes, she'll go very far.

Yes, yes, hmmm.

Make a wish.

A wish?

Yes, make a wish. What do you want?

Anything? I said.

Well, why not?

I closed my eyes.

Did you wish already?

Yes, I said.

Well, that's all there is to it. It'll come true.

How do you know? I asked.

We know, we know.

Esperanza. The one with marble hands called me aside. Esperanza. She held my face with her blue-veined hands and looked and looked at me. A long silence. When you leave you must remember always to come back, she said.

What?

When you leave you must remember to come back for the others. A circle, understand? You will always be Esperanza.

You will always be Mango Street. You can't erase what you know. You can't forget who you are.

Then I didn't know what to say. It was as if she could read my mind, as if she knew what I had wished for, and I felt ashamed for having made such a selfish wish.

You must remember to come back. For the ones who cannot leave as easily as you. You will remember? She asked as if she was telling me. Yes, yes, I said a little confused.

Good, she said, rubbing my hands. Good. That's all. You can go.

I got up to join Lucy and Rachel who were already outside waiting by the door, wondering what I was doing talking to three old ladies who smelled like cinnamon. I didn't understand everything they had told me. I turned around. They smiled and waved in their smoky way.

Then I didn't see them. Not once, or twice, or ever again.

Alicia & I Talking on Edna's Steps

I like Alicia because once she gave me a little leather purse with the word GUADALAJARA stitched on it, which is home for Alicia, and one day she will go back there. But today she is listening to my sadness because I don't have a house.

You live right here, 4006 Mango, Alicia says and points to the house I am ashamed of.

No, this isn't my house I say and shake my head as if shaking could undo the year I've lived here. I don't belong. I don't ever want to come from here. You have a home, Alicia, and one day you'll go there, to a town you remember, but me I never had a house, not even a photograph . . . only one I dream of.

No, Alicia says. Like it or not you are Mango Street, and one day you'll come back too.

Not me. Not until somebody makes it better.

Who's going to do it? The mayor?

And the thought of the mayor coming to Mango Street makes me laugh out loud.

Who's going to do it? Not the mayor.

A House of My Own

Not a flat. Not an apartment in back. Not a man's house. Not a daddy's. A house all my own. With my porch and my pillow, my pretty purple petunias. My books and my stories. My two shoes waiting beside the bed. Nobody to shake a stick at. Nobody's garbage to pick up after.

Only a house quiet as snow, a space for myself to go, clean as paper before the poem.

Mango Says Goodbye Sometimes

I like to tell stories. I tell them inside my head. I tell them after the mailman says, Here's your mail. Here's your mail he said.

I make a story for my life, for each step my brown shoe takes. I say, "And so she trudged up the wooden stairs, her sad brown shoes taking her to the house she never liked."

I like to tell stories. I am going to tell you a story about a girl who didn't want to belong.

We didn't always live on Mango Street. Before that we lived on Loomis on the third floor, and before that we lived on Keeler. Before Keeler it was Paulina, but what I remember most is Mango Street, sad red house, the house I belong but do not belong to.

I put it down on paper and then the ghost does not ache so much. I write it down and Mango says goodbye sometimes. She does not hold me with both arms. She sets me free.

One day I will pack my bags of books and paper. One day I will say goodbye to Mango. I am too strong for her to keep me here forever. One day I will go away.

Friends and neighbors will say, What happened to that Esperanza? Where did she go with all those books and paper? Why did she march so far away?

They will not know I have gone away to come back. For the ones I left behind. For the ones who cannot out.